How to Stop Smoking — Permanently

How to Stop Smoking
— *Permanently*

With the New Nicotine Gum

Walter S. Ross

Foreword by Julius B. Richmond, M.D.
Director, Division of Health Policy Research
& Education, Harvard University
Former Surgeon General,
U.S. Public Health Service

Little, Brown and Company · Boston · Toronto

B

Portions of this book have
appeared in *Reader's Digest*
in slightly different form.

*Nicorette gum is a prescription drug.
You should consult your physician before using it.*

Previously copyrighted material is quoted by permission of the following:

"Do You Know What Happens When You Smoke" (July 1972), "Can Nicotine Help Smokers Quit?" (February 1981), "What Happens When a Smoker Stops" (October 1982), and "Nicotine Gum: The Drug That Helps Smokers Quit" (June 1984), adapted by permission of *Reader's Digest*.

"How You Feel About Quitting" by Tom Wicker, *The New York Times,* January 13, 1984. Copyright © by The New York Times Company. Reprinted by permission.

Two graphs from "Plasma Nicotine Levels Produced by Chewing Nicotine Gum" by McKendree E. McNabb, M.D., et al., *Journal of the American Medical Association* 1982, 248:865-868. Reprinted by permission of the author.

LIBRARY OF CONGRESS CATALOGING IN PUBLICATION DATA

Ross, Walter Sanford, 1916–
  How to stop smoking — permanently.

  1. Cigarette habit.   I. Title.
RC567.R67   1984   616.86'506   84-19411
ISBN 0-316-75752-7

BP

DESIGNED BY DEDE CUMMINGS

*Published simultaneously in Canada
by Little, Brown & Company (Canada) Limited*

PRINTED IN THE UNITED STATES OF AMERICA

This book is dedicated to the thirty-three million Americans who have attempted to quit smoking, to the sixteen million who would like to try, and to the thirty-four million who have been able to stop.

"As a new Fellow of ACCP and a leader in the most important struggle faced by chest physicians, the prevention and control of our major health problems of lung cancer, cardiovascular and chronic pulmonary disease, I shall make a special personal effort to control smoking and to eliminate this hazard from my office, clinic and hospital. I shall ask all of my patients about their smoking habits and I shall assist the cigarette smoker in stopping smoking. I make this pledge to my patients and to society."

— from the Fellowship Pledge of the American College of Chest Physicians

Foreword

SINCE the landmark Surgeon General's report of 1964, the percentage of smokers in our population has declined by about one-third. While this is encouraging, much remains to be done, as this book suggests.

About 53 million of our people still smoke cigarettes these days. Surveys tell us that nearly all wish that they could stop. They need every bit of help they can get. For it's now recognized by science and medicine that smoking cigarettes is perhaps the most addictive and certainly the most frequent and widespread drug-taking habit in this country.

There's no longer any question that the addictive element is nicotine.

A great deal has been learned about this substance, including how to use it to help a large number of smokers break their addiction. This book sums up the latest research in a practical four-step program that permits each smoker to understand and deal with smoking cessation in his/her own way and at his or her own tempo. It also contains the latest information on how to handle the inevitable problems of relapse.

It is not my habit to endorse products or programs for which I am not responsible. But I do not hesitate to recommend this book to smokers who want to quit. My reason is that as Surgeon General of the United States Public Health Service, the smoking problem in this country was one of my major priorities — as it has been with every Surgeon General since the famous *Report on Smoking and Health* of Dr. Luther Terry's Advisory Committee. And it still is.

Smoking cigarettes is the leading *controllable* cause of morbidity and mortality in our environment, responsible for about 375,000 excess or premature deaths each year in the United States. These include about 100,000 deaths from lung cancer and 170,000 from heart attacks. Thus, it is the obvious duty of every public health officer — in fact, of every health care professional — to do all they can to eliminate what we regard as the largest preventable cause of death in this country.

That is the purpose of this book; and since it is soundly based in medicine and science, I have no hesitancy in commending it to the attention of every smoker who wants to fight the addiction.

JULIUS B. RICHMOND, M.D.
Director, Division of Health Policy Research & Education
HARVARD UNIVERSITY
Former Surgeon General,
U.S. PUBLIC HEALTH SERVICE

Contents

How to Stop Smoking — Permanently

Pur<u>pose</u>

It will be necessary to leave off Tobacco. But I had some thoughts of doing that before, for I sometimes think it does not agree with me.

— CHARLES LAMB, *Letter to Wordsworth*

THIRTY-THREE million American smokers have tried to quit and feel, incorrectly as we'll see, that they've failed. Sixteen million more, surveys tell us, would like to try. They are usually afraid to make the attempt because they hold the outdated belief that quitting is just too painful and difficult. They don't know that science and medicine have now made it possible to stop smoking quickly and painlessly.

In fact, there has been a revolution in understanding smoking "cessation," or quitting, in the past few years, and in helping ex-smokers to stay off cigarettes permanently.

Smoking cigarettes was once considered merely a bad habit, forbidden to children but okay for grownups. Then, starting in the 1950s, it was identified as the major cause of lung cancer in the United States and other developed countries. Smoking cigarettes has since been pinpointed as the number-one environmental cause of all U.S. cancer (not only lung cancer, but a half-dozen other tumors as well), of at least 30 percent of heart attack deaths, and of the crippling and killing diseases known collectively as Chronic Obstructive Pulmonary Disease. Practically all smokers are aware of at least some of these dangers. However, even though they may have been scared to death of their habit, the fact that very few could give it up was seen by experts, until quite recently, as a "psychological dependence."

It was certainly widely known that nicotine was in tobacco. And scientists were aware that the drug was psychoactive (it affected mood) and had a variety of physical effects. But no authority would say that it was addictive. Only in the past few years have the American Psychiatric Association and the National Institute on Drug Abuse officially identified smoking as a true addiction in the majority of cigarette smokers, a physiological dependence on nicotine complete with withdrawal symptoms similar to that of narcotics. Like any drug addiction, it becomes embedded in a tangle of chemical craving, emotional need, and lifestyle — that is to say, social reinforcement.

Nicotine is even more addictive than many hard drugs. It is a fact that 50 percent of heroin addicts in the U.S. armed forces were able to kick their habit without help after Vietnam. Yet a group of three hundred opiate addicts in London said that they could more easily give up heroin than cigarettes.

Putting cigarettes in the same category as hard drugs has led to new and more effective ways to help smokers quit. Experts, now convinced that cigarette smokers have been unwittingly incarcerated in an addicts' prison, have developed new techniques, new materials and new approaches to parole smokers from their life sentence.

This book sums up the most advanced knowledge of what smoking is, how and why it addicts or habituates, or causes dependence, and shows you in four simple steps how to break your addiction, habit, or dependence. It will help you mobilize your motivation to quit, by giving you new understanding of the kind of smoker you are, what smoking means to you, how you really feel about quitting (are you serious about wanting to stop?), how your own personal universe can surround you with support or may work against your quitting and staying quit. A simple test tells you how addicted to nicotine you are.

How to Stop Smoking — Permanently tells you a lot you have probably never known about both the dangers of smoking and the benefits of quitting. It introduces you to the first available prescription medication to help smokers quit. This is a true chemical breakthrough, enabling them to overcome the withdrawal symptoms that have frustrated so many who wanted to give up cigarettes. Last, but perhaps most important, the final chapters tell you what to expect in the way of physical effects and mood changes after you quit smoking, and how to deal with these; and to anticipate and master the social and psychological problems encountered by nearly all ex-smokers.

There is no law that says you have to give up cigarettes. If they didn't provide a variety of pleasures and satisfactions and fill an enormous number of needs, more than fifty million American adults wouldn't be smoking them.

But remember that it wasn't easy to learn how to smoke. At first, probably, you were sick; certainly you didn't like the taste. It took months for you to enjoy cigarettes, then to need them. And it's likely taken years for the habit to twine itself into the patterns of your life — your leisure, your pleasure, your pains, your triumphs, your meals, digestion, cocktail hours and coffee breaks; your lovemaking, frustrations, depressions, work and play.

You started smoking because of something that happened to you. There are bound to be similarities with the way other smokers started, but your addiction and theirs are not the same. And you presumably want to stop, or you wouldn't be reading this. Quitting, too, is going to be personal.

But there are common denominators in quitting that this

book can teach you to use, to smooth the way between smoking and nonsmoking.

It's now known that everyone who stops smoking goes through certain phases. The time frame will vary, so there's no point in deciding in advance how long this may take you. (In most cases, we're not talking about months, only days or weeks.) Some people are more strongly motivated, react more quickly, and move faster than others. You can speed-read through this book and gallop through the quitting process. Or you may want to study and ponder, postpone deciding to quit until you feel more comfortable about it. That's why this book is divided into steps, rather than periods of time. But no matter how long you may want to take, it will be easier, and far less irksome, to follow the path shown to you by research and to walk in the footsteps of those who have succeeded, rather than hack your own way through trial and error.

Step · One

Mobilize
Your Motivation

1.

It Isn't a Question of Willpower

*M*OST people think that giving up cigarettes is the result of a conscious decision, that it takes enormous willpower and that it is a single, courageous act. Actually, all these suppositions are unfounded.

· The vast majority of people who have quit smoking permanently have been working at it for months or years, usually without realizing it. In fact, a new study of three thousand smokers at the University of Ottawa shows that the best predictor of permanent quitting is *having tried to quit three to five times*. That is, the people who give up smoking and don't start again are those who have already stopped and "relapsed" an average of that many times. So, anyone who has given up smoking for a day, a week, or months, and gone back to it should have no sense of failure. It is the feeling of impotence stemming from that false perception that keeps so many from trying again, and succeeding.

· Quitting isn't an act, it's a process. Just knowing that fact helps a lot of smokers to overcome the sense of failure that previous aborted attempts usually leave. And now they've got the pharmacological support of a new prescription drug that does for nicotine addicts what methadone does for people addicted to heroin. It's something you can keep with you and use as often as you wish, whenever you are tempted, or you want or crave a cigarette. As a matter of fact, it's been shown that the people who use the product (a chewing gum that gives smokers nicotine without smoking) the longest — for three months — are most likely to be off cigarettes at the end of a year.

· It's also untrue that quitting requires an enormous effort of will. What it takes is organized motivation. The first of our four steps will tell you how to organize your motivations. It will teach you things you never knew about smoking, and about your own habit. This knowledge will give you power: a force to help deliver you to the land of freedom — freedom from tobacco.

2

What Happens When You Smoke

*J*OHN A. Yacenda, who used to run a quit-smoking clinic for the Ventura, California, health department, said that the question most often asked by teenagers is "How long does it take for smoking to harm you?" The reason: Many youngsters have been smoking for just a short time, or smoke only a few cigarettes a day.

Yacenda's answer: "About three seconds." Or less. In the tiny interval after you light a cigarette and start inhaling smoke, the rich country flavor begins to satisfy — by corroding the delicate membranes of your lips and palate, as well as your throat, larynx, pharynx, esophagus. It rasps your lungs, attacks your circulation, your heart, your whole body. Nicotine begins to rush directly into your bloodstream through the gossamer-thin walls of your lungs and in only *seven seconds* a "bolus" — a wallop — passes through the left side of the heart and hits your brain, twice as fast as mainlining heroin. Inhaled nicotine starts your heart pounding from fifteen to twenty-five beats per minute faster; your blood pressure goes up by ten to twenty points. In your lungs, smoke chokes the airways and attacks the air sacs, leaving a residue of cancer-causing chemicals, some of which are radioactive. (A pack-a-day smoker gets the equivalent of several chest X-rays a year.) These and other dangerous compounds are also deposited in your stomach, kidneys, bladder. All this happens with *every* cigarette you smoke; no smoker is immune.

And when you exhale, up to 90 percent of that true tobacco taste stays with you — in the form of billions of microscopic and submicroscopic particles of about four thousand different chemicals. In this balanced blend of fine aromas are acids, glycerol, glycol, alcohols, aldehydes, ketones, aliphatic and aromatic hydrocarbons, phenols. None is a health food; many will do you harm.

For years some scientists scoffed that it wasn't possible for one substance — smoke — to attack so many parts of the body in so many ways. Research has proved, however, that tobacco smoke isn't a single substance. About 92 percent of the country-fresh flavor you inhale is gas — a dozen different noxious vapors, including acrolein, hydrocyanic acid, nitric oxide, nitrogen dioxide, acetone and ammonia. The first four are considered extremely dangerous; and within the past few years, science has zeroed in on one that's even deadlier: colorless, odorless, lethal carbon monoxide, which makes up about 4 percent of cigarette smoke.

This gas has been identified as contributing to heart attacks and sudden coronary death in smokers by Dr. Wilbert S. Aronow of the University of California. Present in cigarette smoke in a concentration 640 times the safe level permitted in the air of industrial plants, this insidious poison gas has about two hundred times the affinity for red blood cells (hemoglobin) as oxygen — and it's oxygen that red blood cells have been designated by nature to distribute throughout the body. So any inhaled carbon monoxide quickly displaces the oxygen in our blood, forming "carboxyhemoglobin." Cigarettes aren't the only source of carbon monoxide; the gas is in automobile exhausts and other smoke, too. So a nonsmoker normally has between 0.5 percent and 2.0 percent of carbon monoxide in his or her red blood cells. But a cigarette smoker, depending on the brand and how many cigarettes he or she smokes, has between 4 and 15 percent or more of carbon monoxide in red blood cells.

This means that the smoker's red blood cells are carrying five to ten times more life-denying carbon monoxide than normal.

Carbon monoxide not only prevents red cells from picking up oxygen, it also hinders them from giving it up as fast as your body needs it — which means that a cigarette smoker who lives at sea level is getting as little oxygen as a nonsmoker at 8,000 feet.

There's no age limit on this effect — a teenager tyro smoker may feel winded under mild stress on only five or six cigarettes a day. It's why every smoker who is active in sports will be panting for air more quickly than nonsmoking competitors.

Carbon monoxide is an all-purpose assailant: for example, it cuts down on the amount of oxygen reaching the fetus in a pregnant woman. Thus, the babies of smoking mothers on average weigh six ounces less than those of nonsmokers.

The sharp jolts of nicotine you inhale in cigarette smoke are what give you that lift — they lift your blood pressure, your heart rate and the amount of blood pumped by your heart. They do this by releasing substances known as catecholamines (the main one is adrenaline) into your tissues. Catecholamines push your heart so hard it requires more blood in its coronary arteries to keep up with the demand. Healthy arteries expand to the occasion. But in people with coronary-artery disease, the hardworking heart does not get the additional blood — and in smokers, that blood doesn't carry enough oxygen. This is thought to be the reason why angina (chest pain) attacks are brought on faster in smokers.

And carbon monoxide seems to be nicotine's accomplice in many assaults on the body. Animal studies show that carbon monoxide makes artery walls more permeable to fatty substances. This may be one of the mechanisms leading to the deposit of fatty plaques which narrow arterial passages. The condition is known as atherosclerosis.

The adrenaline released by jolts of inhaled nicotine aids this process by hitting fat cells all over your body, causing them to pour free fatty acids into your blood. Every time you smoke, your blood level of these fatty acids goes up. Elevated levels of fatty acids may also have an accelerated effect on clotting. Too, some studies have shown that platelets, a clotting factor in the blood, become more adhesive in smokers. This suggests a possible explanation of why smokers get so many more heart attacks than nonsmokers — their blood more readily forms clots, which may block coronary arteries and thereby cause a coronary occlusion or heart attack.

Smoking doesn't cause all the heart attacks in the United States. But the Surgeon General calculates that it is responsible for about 170,000 extra, or premature, U.S. heart attack deaths per year.

The flavor and taste you enjoy in your cigarette come mainly from those billions of chemical particles mentioned earlier. Condensed from smoke, they form viscous, smelly tar. A pack-a-day smoker each year inhales up to eight ounces — a full cup — of tar in cigarette smoke.

Even as it pours tar into your lungs, smoke neutralizes their defenses against tar and other hazards. It affects the mucus, which traps dirt and microbes; the cilia, tiny hairlike structures lining the airways, which normally beat steadily to move the mucus toward the throat where it can be coughed up; and macrophages, hardworking, vacuum-cleaner-like cells, which gather and dispose of harmful substances. The cigarette smoke you gulp directly into your lungs produces excess mucus while slowing down and eventually stopping the cilia, and hampering the macrophages' ability to digest or expel foreign matter. Thus, smoke makes lungs more vulnerable to poisons and microbes.

In tar — against which your lungs are prevented from defending themselves — there are at least thirty chemicals known to help cause cancer. Several are "complete carcinogens," which means that they can start malignant tumors all by themselves. One such is beta-naphthylamine, a specific cause of bladder cancer in human beings and so powerful that many countries have restricted its manufacture (it's used in dyes). A medical researcher has calculated that 35 percent of bladder cancers in the United States are caused by cigarettes, resulting in 3,100 deaths a year.

But tar is a more powerful cancer-causing agent than the sum of its parts. Wherever it touches living tissue it produces abnormal cells. These aren't cancer, but it is among these deformed cells that cancers start. In pipe and cigar smokers who generally don't inhale, the common smoking-caused cancer areas are lip, tongue, mouth, larynx and esophagus. In cigarette smokers, who almost always do inhale, the excess cancers include all the above plus lung, bladder and pancreas.

Even today, lung cancer is so hard to detect at an early, curable stage, that it is about 90 percent fatal. It is the leading site of cancer in men, in the United States, and it's rising so fast among U.S. women that it is expected to surpass breast cancer as their leading malignancy. Lung cancer, about 82 percent the result of smoking, will cause a total of about 121,000 deaths this year in this country. In fact, a recent Surgeon General's report calculates that cigarette smoking is responsible for about 30 percent of *all* cancers in the United States.

Cigarettes also cause other lung diseases, which permit you to smoke yourself to death more slowly and painfully than if you get lung cancer. Most smokers know well that first-thing-in-the-morning coughing spell. It starts the day because during the night your anesthetized cilia begin to wake up and move the mucus. You're forced to cough to get rid of it. As smoking continues, this cough becomes chronic. Steady hacking and spitting are the symptoms of chronic bronchitis. Overproduction of mucus caused by this disease provides a breeding ground for bacteria, while reducing the lungs' ability to fight off infection — one reason why smokers get more colds and other respiratory infections. Chronic bronchitis is more than just a chronic cough; it can also lead to death.

Chronic bronchitis and its steady companion, emphysema — of which the Surgeon General says cigarettes are the most important cause — kill more than 30,000 Americans, and cause the loss of more than thirty-five million man-days of work each year. There is good reason to believe that 99 percent of cigarette smokers who smoke more than a pack a day have some emphysema, a disease that destroys the lungs' air sacs. (Pathologist Dr. Oscar Auerbach studied the lungs of some 1,800 deceased men and women whose smoking histories were known, and classified them — without knowing whose lungs he was examining — by the amount of emphysema that he could see. Matching the lung tissues with the smoking histories of the patients, he found that more than 99 percent of those who had smoked twenty or more cigarettes daily had the disease, and in 19 percent it was far advanced; 90 percent of the nonsmokers had no emphysema and there wasn't a single advanced case among them.) Even among coal miners and others exposed to lung-damaging dust, smoking plays a significant part in death from emphysema.

"Lung cancer is a comparatively merciful death," says one doctor. "With emphysema you start gasping and you may gasp for fifteen years." It creeps up on smokers. We all start with about one hundred square yards of interior lung surface. But we almost never need all of this; most of us live on a small part, about 20 percent of it. The first hint a smoker gets of emphysema is usually when he finds himself out of breath after a minor exertion. He may think that this is an early warning; it isn't. It means that most of his 80 percent of lung reserve has been destroyed.

Even after a warning like this, many smokers bravely refuse to give up cigarettes until it is too late. Visit the respiratory ward of your local hospital, and you'll see these poor wretches never more than a few yards from their oxygen tanks and respirators, their entire lives focused on a single act: breathing.

The litany of smoking-related diseases does not stop here. Smokers have more gastric ulcers than nonsmokers, and take longer to heal; more periodontal disease, which attacks teeth and gums, and more trench mouth; more severe upper respiratory infections, which last longer than in nonsmokers. There is evidence that it diminishes male fertility, that there is somehow a connection with cervical (neck of the womb) cancer in women, and that smokers have poorer hearing than nonsmokers. There is even an eye disease caused by smoking: it's called tobacco ambylopia. This means partial loss of sight, without any obvious damage to the retina or optic nerve.

Smoking is also linked with osteoporosis: loss of calcium from bones, a very serious problem in women after menopause. This is a major cause of bone fractures that eventually cripple many women. Smokers have lower blood levels of vitamin C than nonsmokers, and their bodies don't benefit from this vitamin as much as those of nonsmokers. Smoking also interferes with vitamin B_{12} metabolism. Studies indicate that cigarette smoke attacks the central nervous system, that is, the brain and spinal cord, in a variety of ways. The major effects on mood and mental ability, as well as reaction time, are summed up in the chapter on nicotine, starting on page 51.

The damage is "dose related." Each cigarette does some harm. Each additional smoke repeats the insult. A pack-a-day smoker inhales smoke about 50,000 to 70,000 times a year. Eventually these incessant attacks on the body may turn into disease. After about a million puffs, or 100,000 cigarettes — perhaps a pack a day for fifteen years — smokers begin to edge into the lung-cancer danger zone.

There is no such thing as a safe level of smoking; no such thing as a safe cigarette. ("The only safe cigarette is one that hasn't been smoked," said Dr. Gio Gori, former head of cigarette research at the National Cancer Institute.) But since the harm is dose related, research shows that cutting down on the number of cigarettes smoked, smoking those with efficient filters and less tar and nicotine, will somewhat reduce — or postpone — the risk of serious illness. Providing you don't cancel the benefit by smoking more, inhaling more deeply, or more often. However, as we'll see later, studies show that cutting down is not the way to go for people who really want to avoid the dangers of smoking. The only certain way to do that — and, for the great majority of smokers, the easiest way — is to quit.

What happens when you do? First, your chronic bronchitis begins to clear up: no more hacking and coughing. Fewer and less severe colds. A cleaner mouth and breath. Stay off cigarettes for a year and your risk of heart attack goes down sharply. Keep it up for two years, and you begin to move out of the high-risk lung cancer area. The symptoms of emphysema may even improve — in any case, they will stop getting worse — although the lung tissue destroyed by smoke will not regenerate.

The thing to remember is that when you stop insulting your lungs with air that tastes good like a cigarette should, whatever breathing capacity you have left, you'll *keep*.

Dangers of Smoking Cigarettes	*Benefits of Quitting*
Two-pack-a-day smokers *die, on the average, about 8.3 years younger* than nonsmokers. Smokers of more or fewer cigarettes have proportional mortality risk.	*Risk drops daily*; After 10 to 15 years, it is close to that of those who never smoked.
Major risk of coronary heart disease: Cigarette smoking is responsible for at least 170,000 excess U.S. heart attack deaths each year.	*Risk drops sharply* after one year; at 10 years, about same as someone who has never smoked.
Smoking is a direct *cause of about 100,000 U.S. lung cancer deaths a year* in both men and women, and rising.	*Risk recedes steadily*, down to normal after 10 to 15 years.
Bronchitis/Emphysema: Risk of death from these diseases is four to twenty-five times as high as in nonsmokers.	*Cough, excess sputum disappear in a few weeks; lung function improves, deterioration stops.*

(Continued)

Dangers of Smoking Cigarettes	*Benefits of Quitting*
Pregnant women have higher risk of *miscarriage, stillbirth, low birthweight infants*; the latter results in more infant disease and death.	*Extra risk imposed by smoking disappears when smoking stops.*
Children of smoking mothers may be *retarded in physical/mental development.*	*Not smoking during pregnancy avoids this unnecessary risk.*
Overall, smokers of tobacco in any form have from three to seventeen times as much *larynx cancer* as nonsmokers.	*Steady reduction of risk*, returns to normal after 10 years.
All smokers — pipe, cigar, cigarettes — have very high risk of *mouth cancer*. Those who drink alcohol multiply the risk.	Eliminating smoking/drinking *gradually eliminates this additional risk* over 10 to 15 years.
Smokers have two to nine times the risk of *esophageal cancer* as nonsmokers. Alcohol drinkers who smoke have greatly increased risk.	Since risk of smoking/drinking is synergistic (multiplying) and dose related, *stopping both eliminates risk factors.*

(Continued)

Dangers of Smoking Cigarettes	*Benefits of Quitting*
Risk of *bladder cancer* is seven to ten times that of nonsmokers. Risk increases if smokers are exposed to dyes or other chemicals.	*Risk drops to that of non-smokers after 7 years.*
Pancreatic cancer: there is two to five times the risk of death from this cancer for smokers than for nonsmokers.	*Since risk is dose related, eliminating smoking should eliminate risk.*
Smokers have more *peptic ulcers*, greater risk of death from them, and heal poorly after treatment.	*No-smoking eliminates risk factor;* ex-smokers get ulcers, but they heal faster.
Smokers have more *allergies* and the *immune system is impaired*.	Since these are directly related to smoking, *stopping eliminates related risks.*
Effects of medicines, diagnostic tests (diabetes) are altered; greatly increased risk of strokes and heart attacks in users of oral contraceptives.	Levels of majority of blood components deranged by smoking return to normal on cessation, *eliminating adverse drug and test effects; risk of blood clots (strokes, heart attacks, thrombophlebitis) in ex-smoking Pill-takers drops sharply.*

Step · Two

Analyze Your Own Smoking

3

Know
Your Own Habit

*A lone man's companion, a bachelor's friend, a hungry
man's food, a sad man's cordial, a wakeful man's sleep,
and a chilly man's fire. Sir, for stanching of wounds,
purging of rheum, and settling of the stomach, there's
no herb like unto it under the canopy of heaven.*

— CHARLES KINGSLEY
Westward Ho!

*B*EFORE you quit, it's helpful to know *what kind* of smoker
you are. The more you understand your habit patterns, the
easier it is to rearrange them.

Following is a self test. Fill out the questionnaire unless
you're certain that you know everything about why you
smoke. The test will take you only a minute or two. At the
end is a system of scoring yourself, and a method of as-
sessing your own particular smoking habit. Circle the number that comes closest to your own practice.

For an accurate score, answer all questions:

TEST I   *What Kind of Smoker Are You?*

	Always	Often	Sometimes	Seldom	Never
A. I smoke cigarettes to keep from slowing down.	5	4	3	2	1
B. Handling cigarettes is part of the pleasure of smoking.	5	4	3	2	1
C. Smoking is pleasant and relaxing.	5	4	3	2	1
D. I smoke when I feel angry	5	4	3	2	1
E. If I run out of cigarettes I can't wait to buy some.	5	4	3	2	1
F. Sometimes I smoke without even knowing it.	5	4	3	2	1
G. Smoking gives me a lift.	5	4	3	2	1
H. It's fun just to light up.	5	4	3	2	1
I. Cigarettes are pleasurable.	5	4	3	2	1
J. I smoke when I'm irritated or upset.	5	4	3	2	1

TEST I *What Kind of Smoker Are You? (continued)*

	Always	Often	Sometimes	Seldom	Never
K. I'm uncomfortably aware of when I'm not smoking.	5	4	3	2	1
L. Sometimes I light a cigarette unaware that one is already burning in the ashtray.	5	4	3	2	1
M. Smoking is stimulating.	5	4	3	2	1
N. I like to watch the smoke when I exhale.	5	4	3	2	1
O. I want a cigarette most when I'm comfortable and relaxed.	5	4	3	2	1
P. When I'm blue I smoke to forget care and worry.	5	4	3	2	1
Q. I get a real craving to smoke when I haven't smoked for a while.	5	4	3	2	1
R. I've found a cigarette in my mouth without remembering putting it there.	5	4	3	2	1

How to score Test I

Enter the number you've selected for each question next to the letter below that identifies the question. Thus, the number for question A goes next to letter A, the number you've chosen for question G goes next to the letter G, and so on. Then add the three numbers *horizontally* on each line and write the total for that line next to the word at the end of the line — "Stimulation," "Handling," and the like — in the column headed by "Totals."

The Total for each line will be from three to 15. Any sum of 11 or more is significant for the particular category. Any score of seven or less is not considered a strong indicator.

For every score of 11 or more read the paragraph corresponding to the word next to your score, e.g. "Stimulation," "Handling," and so on:

Totals

A	G	M	*Stimulation*
B	H	N	*Handling*
C	I	O	*Relaxation*
D	J	P	*Tension Reduction*
E	K	Q	*Addiction*
F	L	R	*Habit*

As you can see, the test enables you to score yourself on six different reasons for smoking. Don't be surprised if you have several scores above 11. Most people smoke for more than one reason, and the combinations differ.

The first three categories are positive reasons for smoking. The second group are negative. And knowing in which categories you score highest will have some impact on how you'll most easily quit smoking.

Stimulation. A high stimulation score means you get a sense of increased energy from smoking. You're likely to begin the day with a cigarette. You may want to smoke more when you feel tired, and you get a kick out of smoking.

Handling. Smoking is something to occupy your hands. You have certain rituals about smoking — the kind of pack you prefer, the way you take out the cigarette, the way you light it and what you use — a lighter, matches — and you probably enjoy watching the smoke, perhaps blowing smoke rings, exhaling through your nose.

Relaxation. A large number of smokers say that cigarettes relax them. This may be because they've conditioned themselves to smoke when they are relaxed. Is this true of you? The effect may also be physiological: nicotine is a paradoxical drug that may be both stimulating and depressing at different times in the same person. See the nicotine chapter starting on page 51 for an explanation of this phenomenon.

If you smoke for relaxation, chances are you most enjoy smoking after a meal or a cocktail, or coffee. Used this way, cigarettes are a kind of reward, a means of enhancing pleasure.

The negative reasons for smoking are:

Tension Reduction. If you score high here, you use cigarettes less for pleasure than to avoid pain — to reduce tension, stress, anxiety, anger. At least 30 percent of smokers use cigarettes this way — but not necessarily exclusively for these purposes.

Addiction. People who crave a smoke, usually need one at least every 30 minutes. Do you smoke this often, particularly at work or under tension? If you feel that something is missing when you're not smoking — if you wake up at

night needing to smoke — if, when you run out of cigarettes, you'll go out in a rainstorm to buy some — you're
really hooked on nicotine. And this is not necessarily bad
news, as you'll see in the chapter starting on page 65, "Nicotine Can Help You Quit." Experts estimate that a majority
of smokers fall into this group.

Habit. Although cigarette smoking is a habit, dependence, or addiction, or a combination of all three, the habit
smoker is someone special. If you score high here, smoking
has become almost an unconscious act; you may often smoke
without realizing it. Former U.S. President Dwight D. Eisenhower was that kind of smoker. When he lit a cigarette
one day and saw one in the ashtray that he'd just lit a minute
before, he got so mad at his habit that he quit. When asked
later if he would ever smoke again, Eisenhower replied,
with a grin, "I don't know. But if I do, I know I'm going
to quit again." The true habit smoker often doesn't enjoy
smoking, just buys and burns packs of cigarettes because
he or she doesn't know what to do without them. That's
something you'll learn from this book.

4

How You Feel About Smoking

TEST II *How Do You Feel About Smoking?*

This test is similar in format to Test I, but it will show you something different — not what kind of smoker you are, but what you know and feel about smoking in general. This, too, is an important aid to quitting. As in Test I, you have to answer all the questions to get a meaningful score.

	Strongly Agree	Mildly Agree	Mildly Disagree	Strongly Disagree
A. Cigarette smoking is as dangerous as many other health hazards.	1	2	3	4

(continued)

	Strongly Agree	Mildly Agree	Mildly Disagree	Strongly Disagree
B. I don't smoke enough to get any disease smoking is supposed to cause.	1	2	3	4
C. I've been smoking so long it probably wouldn't do any good to stop.	1	2	3	4
D. It would be very pain-ful to give up cigarettes.	1	2	3	4
E. Cigarette smoking is enough of a health hazard to warrant doing something to stop it.	1	2	3	4
F. My brand is much less likely to cause any smok-ing-related disease.	1	2	3	4
G. As soon as someone quits smoking, the body begins to repair itself.	1	2	3	4
H. I don't think I could cut my smoking by one-half.	1	2	3	4
I. The so-called health risks of smoking are only statistics.	1	2	3	4

	Strongly Agree	Mildly Agree	Mildly Disagree	Strongly Disagree
J. I haven't smoked long enough to worry about any smoking disease.	1	2	3	4
K. Quitting smoking prolongs your life.	1	2	3	4
L. It would be hard to change my smoking habits.	1	2	3	4

HOW TO SCORE YOURSELF

Scoring is similar to that in Test I. Enter the number you have chosen as a reply to each question next to the letter below designating that question. Add the numbers horizontally and put the total next to the word that goes with that line — "Importance, Personal Relevance," etc.

Totals

A	E	I	Importance
B	F	J	Personal Relevance
C	G	K	Benefits of Stopping
D	H	L	Ability to Stop

Any score of six or less is considered below the level of significance — meaning that this category does not apply, or applies only marginally, to you. Scores between six and nine mean that these categories are of intermediate relevance to your attitudes. On the other hand, a score of nine or above means a good deal in terms of your attitudes toward smoking.

Importance. A high score shows that you are aware of the serious health risks of smoking. Many smokers know something of these, but ignore them for various reasons. Many wait until they get a serious smoking-related illness — like a heart attack, or lung cancer. Then, they find it quite easy to stop smoking, but it may be too late. You can strengthen your motivation to quit if you seriously consider all the hazards while you've still got your health. It won't take long.

Suggestions: Read, or reread, Chapter 3, "What Happens When You Smoke," and go over the chart on pages 20–22, "Dangers of Smoking, Benefits of Quitting."

Personal Relevance. A score of nine or above means that you have a strong motive for quitting smoking. A lower score, on the other hand, probably means that you think that smoking may harm others, but not you, or that you haven't been smoking long enough to be hurt. Disabusing yourself of these notions gives you points toward quitting.

Betting that cigarettes won't harm you is very much like playing Russian roulette with live ammunition. Some people can smoke for a lifetime without getting sick from it. But the odds are heavily against you. And there's no way of knowing if you're going to be lucky. Remember, you're betting your life and health against a bad habit — and one that's relatively easy and painless to give up.

Benefits of Stopping. A high score tells you that you are very aware of the benefits of quitting smoking; a low one means that you need either more information or a better understanding of what you've been hearing and reading about this.

You should know that good things start to happen the day you quit. First is an improved sense of taste and smell (and you'll smell a lot better to others, as well). No more burned spots on your clothes or furniture. You'll save money every day (on average, about $1.50 for the typical smoker). Your extra risk of heart attack — smoking is one of three major risk factors in heart attack, the others are high blood pressure and high cholesterol — begins dropping, and is practically gone after a year. All excess illness risks decline at varying rates, and so does the excess risk of premature death that haunts every smoker.

Ability to Stop. A high score indicates that you will probably have no problem. A low score means that you think you can't get along without cigarettes. Fact is, among people who have quit smoking permanently, you can find many who thought as you do — and who, perhaps, were heavier, more addicted smokers. And many did it at a time when there was no nicotine chewing gum to break the chemical addiction, and before the new psychological information on avoiding relapse existed. It was really difficult for them. It's going to be very easy for you.

5

How You Feel
About Quitting

Labor Day 1966 lives in my memory. That morning I woke up coughing, hacking and spewing as usual, reaching with palsied hand for a cigarette. As my yellow-tipped fingers closed around the pack, somewhere in my shriveled interior a contemptuous voice whispered hoarsely;

What a ridiculous condition for a grown man to get himself into!

I slumped back to my pillow, much as Saul of Tarsus must have fallen to earth on the road to Damascus. With sudden loathing I gazed at the bedside ashtray, overflowing with the foul detritus of addiction and folly, and whispered a vow to the stale blue air:

Never again!

I was then a two-pack-daily smoker by admission, and nearer three in private practice. Fancying myself a writer, I nevertheless could not coax a, *and,* or *the* out *of the typewriter without first lighting up, and not uncommonly, when in the throes of literature, I found myself with one cigarette in hand, another in the ashtray, and a third perched on the edge of the desk — all burning like bombs.*

In the Kennedy White House, where I served time as a correspondent, I took up cigars in imitation of the President and press secretary. Later I switched to the cheap cigarillo, thin and deadly as a krait. . . . If spittoons had stayed in fashion, I'd have chewed the stuff (and in fact did in my youthful baseball days).

*Despite that history, and with the aid of several car-
tons of Life Savers and uncounted gallons of black
coffee, I shook the habit in three days, cold turkey. On
the morning of the fourth day I propounded Wicker's
Iron Law of Redemption: If you want to stop smoking,
you can. If you merely think you ought to, you're kid-
ding yourself.*

> — TOM WICKER
> ASSOCIATE EDITOR AND COLUMNIST
> *The New York Times*
> JANUARY 13, 1983

T HE third dimension in quitting is understanding how you
feel about it. There are five basic reasons that impel most
smokers to stop. The following quiz will reveal to you which
of these are most powerful in your own decision.

TEST III   *How You Feel About Quitting*

As with other quizzes, answer all questions (by circling the
appropriate numbers) even if they seem obvious or repetitive.

	Extremely Important	Rather Important	Fairly Unimportant	Don't Care
A. Smoking might give me a serious disease.	4	3	2	1
B. My smoking sets a bad example.	4	3	2	1

	Extremely Important	Rather Important	Fairly Unimportant	Don't Care
C. Cigarette smoking is a messy habit.	4	3	2	1
D. Stopping smoking is a challenge to me.	4	3	2	1
E. Cigarettes are too expensive.	4	3	2	1
F. Smoking makes me short of breath.	4	3	2	1
G. If I quit smoking, others might follow my example.	4	3	2	1
H. Cigarettes burn my clothes, rugs, furniture.	4	3	2	1
I. Quitting smoking demonstrates self-control.	4	3	2	1
J. Quitting would save me $550 a year after taxes.	4	3	2	1
K. If I don't stop smoking, it will make me sick.	4	3	2	1

	Extremely Important	Rather Important	Fairly Unimportant	Don't Care
L. Children who see me smoke are encouraged to smoke.	4	3	2	1
M. When I quit, my senses of taste and smell will improve.	4	3	2	1
N. I hate the idea of being controlled by a habit.	4	3	2	1
O. Smoking is like setting fire to money.	4	3	2	1

How to score yourself

Scoring is the same as for the previous quizzes in this book. Enter the numbers you have circled next to the letter corresponding to the question you have answered. Add the numbers horizontally across, and write the total of each line at the right, next to the word at the end of the line: "Health," "Example" and so on.

Totals

A	F	K	Health
B	G	L	Example
C	H	M	Aesthetics
D	I	N	Control
E	J	O	Expense

The total for each line can vary from three to twelve. A score of nine or more on one line means that your motive for quitting is strong. Scores less than six indicate weak motives.

Health.   You've already taken a test on your knowledge of the health hazards of smoking. This test tells you how you feel about these risks. A low score means you don't believe the dangers, or think they don't apply to you because it's "too late" or because you think you can dodge the statistics. Perhaps you should reread the chapter on "What Happens When You Smoke" and ask your doctor what he thinks.

Example.   A high score means that you know you're setting a bad example for young people. They might be your own children, or nieces or nephews. Perhaps you're a teacher, or a health professional — concerned about your image with young patients. Or a Scoutmaster. There are certainly people who look up to you, and tend to follow your example.

The "exemplar" role is the second strongest motive for wanting to quit smoking. If you score high in this category, this is working on your side.

Aesthetics.   Many smokers are concerned about their cigarette breath, their general aroma of stale smoke, stained fingers, burned clothing and furniture, the stale odor of their home. A New Jersey woman was appalled when, after being confined in hospital for several days without smoking, she got a whiff of her nurse's breath. "Do I smell like that when I smoke?" she asked herself. Another women, a secretary in Ventura, California, told me, "I got tired of people calling me 'sir' when I answered the phone; my voice was that hoarse from smoking." Both of these women quit.

Control. Many smokers resent feeling out of control because of a habit that is dominating their lives. A doctor I know quit this way. He was coughing his way down Fifth Avenue in New York City one morning when he realized that his hacking was cigarette-caused. He took out two fresh packs of cigarettes, and a Dunhill lighter, tossed them into the nearest trash can, and never smoked again.

A man in Quebec, Canada, said, "One Sunday night I was going out for cigarettes. My wife said she needed milk for the kids' breakfast. I didn't have enough money for both, and I couldn't cash a check on a Sunday. The fact that I had to think about whether to buy cigarettes or milk suddenly hit me as *sick*. I haven't smoked since."

Expense. The average smoker in the United States consumes 30 cigarettes a day. That's a pack and a half, at about a dollar per pack. In the course of a year, that smoker spends nearly $550 on smoking, *after taxes*. Which means about $700 of earned before-tax income.

That's an expensive habit — not as costly as heroin or cocaine, perhaps, but still enough for most peple to think twice about. There are better things to do with the money — a St. Paul, Minnesota, man, W. J. Kortesmaki, decided to bank the dollars he would have spent on cigarettes (a pack and a half a day) after he quit smoking. Fifteen years later, he took himself, his wife and two teenage daughters on a European vacation on the money he had saved, and the interest it had earned.

An Atlanta, Georgia, woman worked it in reverse: she bought a money order for $730, the amount she would spend in a year for two packs of cigarettes daily. She gave the money order to her husband, and told him that if she smoked within a year, he should cash it and keep the money. She stayed off cigarettes and used the cash to buy clothes.

It may not add to your motivation to quit smoking to know that your smoking costs you, your insurance company, perhaps your employer, your trade union, and the government many thousands of dollars. A recent study by Policy Analysis, a research group in Boston, estimates that on average each pack of cigarettes smoked generates about $3 in costs — for health care and lost wages and production. That is, a one- to two-pack-a-day male smoker, between ages forty and forty-four, will be responsible for an additional $33,000 of such costs during the rest of his life, on average. For women it's considerably less, but substantial. Quitting cuts these wasted expenses by more than half.

CAUTION: Having strong motives for quitting used to create problems for some people. They wanted so badly to quit, without being prepared to do so, and without having the necessary help and support, that they were made anxious. Their desire to quit fed on their anxiety, creating frustration — and this led them to smoke even more. This need no longer be the case, for there is now a pharmacological aid to quitting that was not available (except experimentally) in the United States before 1984. This is the big advantage that current quitters have. Step 3 (page 65) will tell you how this can help you.

6

Your World, Smoking or Nonsmoking?

*A*s a smoker, you must be aware that your world is shrinking. In countries like the United States and in Western Europe, smokers have for some time been in the minority, and their percentage of the population has been dwindling. A recent Gallup survey in the United States indicates that only 29 percent of us over age eighteen are smokers (31 percent men, 28 percent women); twenty years ago, well over 40 percent of the adult population smoked. This is not reported to make you feel threatened. Actually, since you want to quit smoking, these trends are in your favor.

Almost daily the nonsmoking majority passes some new law or ordinance, enforcing its demand for smokeless air in public places. You, like many smokers, may resent these regulations as an intrusion on your liberty. But they may be of positive benefit for someone like yourself who wants to stop smoking and stay quit. Smoke-free airlines, hotels, tours, rent-a-cars, can support your resolve. The more places you can't smoke, the more difficult it is to smoke, the easier it is for you to stop.

The cigarette companies are aware of this, which is why

they spend many millions of dollars fighting antismoking regulations. Already, smoking is *out* among the trend-setters in the population — the same group that popularized cigarette smoking in the 1920s and 1930s. Tobacco manufacturers can't afford to let smoking become an activity restricted to consenting adults, in private. But they're fighting a retreating action, and they know it well. All major U.S. tobacco manufacturers already operate under corporate names in which "tobacco" no longer appears. All are "diversifying" — increasing their investments in enterprises unrelated to smoking: container shipping, industrial solvents, aluminum foil, soft drinks, beer, whiskey and dozens more. "We're preparing to phase out tobacco," one industry executive told me a few years ago. "Not next year, but perhaps in twenty years."

An ominous decline for cigarette marketers is among young men, ages twenty-one to twenty-four, for this is an important group of smokers and a key indicator — the pool upon which the tobacco industry projects future sales. In eleven years recently, the percentage of these younger male smokers dropped from 67 to 41, and the trend is consistently downward. This, too, works to your advantage — fewer smokers means that those who want to smoke may think twice about lighting up. Thinking about not smoking is not what the cigarette manufacturers want you to do.

Various surveys show that more and more smokers would like to kick their habit — the estimates run as high as 95 percent. So you've got plenty of company — a reinforcer for anyone who wants to quit. And surveys by the National Clearinghouse for Smoking and Health have found that the percentage of smokers who have attempted to stop, and succeeded for at least thirty days, has been rising. As many as 85 percent of those who tried were able to stay away from cigarettes for a month or more.

The dramatic increase in the ability to quit doesn't mean only that smokers are more motivated to free themselves of their habit — which seems to be true — but that the cigarettes they are smoking are a lot less addictive than those of a generation ago, therefore easier to give up. For one of the consequences of the drumfire of reports linking smoking with a variety of diseases and a large number of excess deaths has been a soaring demand for "safer" cigarettes. This has resulted in about 95 percent of all U.S. cigarettes now being sold with filter tips; and about 50 percent rated as low in tar and nicotine: less than 15 mgs of tar, and less than 1 mg of nicotine. The total tonnage of tar and nicotine inhaled by U.S. smokers has been dropping even while cigarette sales were rising; and in the past four years, total cigarette sales have been dropping as well in this country.

If past trends had continued, there would be close to eighty million smokers in the United States; instead, there are about fifty-six million. Still, that is a lot of smokers. And cigarettes are still a legal commodity. They can be advertised (although not on TV and radio) and sold almost anywhere in this country and, in spite of laws to protect minors, to almost everybody. Smoking is restricted in more and more public and work places, but it will almost certainly never be prohibited in the United States or any other democratic society. There are still more places where smoking is permitted than prohibited.

So there are conflicting factors in your environment that either encourage you to smoke, or make it easy for you not to do so. You don't see heroes or heroines smoking very often in movies or in TV shows, but your newspaper and magazines are loaded with tobacco advertising (one result of the broadcast ban on cigarette commercials). The U.S. tobacco industry spends more than $1 billion a year perpetuating the social acceptance of smoking, inducing you to smoke. They claim with some justification that cigarette advertising is brand competition; but there is little doubt that its total effect is to create a climate in which smoking is associated with health, sports, beauty and success (in spite of the fact that the cigarette manufacturers promised not to do this in their advertising when the Tobacco Act was passed in 1970).

All that seductive advertising is being bought to influence you and the other fifty-six million smokers, because cigarettes are still the most profitable product of the diversified tobacco companies. They know that an important aspect of your smoking (or quitting) is the kind of world you live in, *and your perception of it.* Does it invite smoking, and is it apt to tempt you to relapse when you quit; or does it offer positive persuasion and reinforcement not to smoke. It's very important to you that you understand the influence of your personal universe on your behavior; that you identify and avoid the social situations, people, and factors that work against quitting, while seeking support for your resolve to give up smoking.

TEST IV *Your World: Smoking or Nonsmoking*

The purpose of this test is to assess the smoking forces that surround you, what they may do to confirm your desire to quit, and what effect they will have on you after you stop smoking. Circle one of the numbers after each of the following questions:

	True or Mostly True	False or Mostly False
A. Doctors have decreased or stopped smoking cigarettes in recent years.	2	1
B. In recent years there seem to be more rules about where you can smoke.	2	1
C. Cigarette ads do not make smoking appear attractive to me.	2	1
D. Schools are trying to discourage children from smoking.	2	1
E. Doctors are trying to get their patients to stop smoking.	2	1
F. Someone recently tried to get me to stop smoking.	2	1
G. Constantly seeing cigarette ads doesn't make it hard for me to quit smoking	2	1
H. The government and health agencies are trying to discourage smoking.	2	1
I. A doctor has talked to me at least once about stopping smoking.	2	1

	True or Mostly True	False or Mostly False
J. It seems that more and more people object to smoking near them.	2	1
K. Cigarette ads do not remind me to smoke.	2	1
L. Congress seems to be concerned about smoking and health.	2	1

M. The people you work with, socialize with, and live with may make it easier or harder for you to smoke. This question can't be phrased as specifically as the others. But you can get an idea of these influences by circling one of the numbers below:

3 They make it much harder to quit smoking
4 They make it somewhat more difficult to quit
5 They make it somewhat easier to quit
6 They make it much easier to stop smoking

How to score yourself:

1. Enter the numbers you have circled for each question next to the appropriate letters below.

2. Total the numbers horizontally on each line. Put the total next to the word at the end of each line, e.g., "Doctors," "General Climate."

Totals

A	E	I	*Doctors*
B	F	J	*General Climate*
C	G	K	*Advertising Influence*

D H L   *Group Influences*

M   *Personal Influences*

Scores vary from three to six on each line. Six is high, five above average, four below average, three low.

Surveys indicate that these five factors play an important part in quitting and not smoking. A low score means that that particular factor may be a barrier in your attempt to quit permanently; a high score tells you that you've got support, or at least no obstacle, in this particular area.

Doctors.   If you are like most people, your doctor's opinion of health matters is a powerful influence on your behavior. And if your doctor is typical of the medical profession, he or she probably believes that smoking is the number-one health problem in the environment, and one controllable by individual decision. Your physician probably does not smoke, even if he/she once did: only about 10 to 20 percent of U.S. M.D.s now smoke — twenty years ago, 80 percent were smokers. A high score shows that you are aware of and probably responsive to medical attitudes toward smoking.

However, your physician may not have advised you about smoking — because it took too much time, the results were often uncertain, and he/she had no real help to give. But doctors can and should help anyone who wants to quit. And, as noted, they now have something effective to prescribe that can help patients stop smoking. **Don't be afraid to ask your doctor for help.**

General Climate.   Since you are a smoker, chances are your environment has been congenial, or at least not hostile to your habit. If this is so, you will score low here, and it will be very useful for you to consciously change your environment as much as possible when you stop smoking. Seek out the company of nonsmokers; you may want to join a quit-smoking group — you can probably find one from your American Cancer Society, or American Lung Association, or American Heart Association, or perhaps your local hospital or county medical society; they are all in the phone book. As much as possible stay away from places where there's a lot of smoking — bars or parties — and go to places where it's prohibited: church, the movies, the public library.

Advertising Influence.   If you score low in this category, you are susceptible to the tacit suggestions in cigarette advertising and are being manipulated by sophisticated techniques. Now that you know this, make a conscious effort to avoid seeing the ads or being influenced by them. Don't read magazines that accept cigarette advertising (more than forty do not, including *The New Yorker, Good Housekeeping, Reader's Digest, National Geographic)*. This advice may be more difficult for a woman to take; almost all women's magazines depend heavily on cigarette advertising to keep themselves profitable.

Group Influences.   We're all influenced by certain groups; if you score high in this area you are aware of and influenced by the attitudes and actions of the federal government, public and private health agencies, schools — all are on record that smoking is harmful, and are trying to do something about it. A low score doesn't necessarily mean that there aren't other influences in your life on your side — perhaps your minister, priest or rabbi, your favorite sports team, some person you don't know but look up to and who doesn't smoke.

Personal Influences.   Almost everybody is sensitive to the opinions, moods, attitudes of certain individuals. As noted, we couldn't be specific here because there are so many possible influences. But if your answer to question "M" is five or six, people who are important to you are likely to be supportive when you quit smoking.

7

How Addicted Are You?
What You Should Know
About Nicotine

Only plants with active pharmacological principles have been employed habitually by large populations over long periods; e.g., tobacco (nicotine); coffee, tea and cocoa (caffeine); betel nut morsel (arecoline); marihuana (cannabis); khat (pseudoephedrine); opium (morphine); coca leaves (cocaine); and others . . .

— SMOKING AND HEALTH — REPORT OF THE ADVISORY COMMITTEE TO THE SURGEON GENERAL OF THE U.S. PUBLIC HEALTH SERVICE

Dr. Sigmund Freud, the founder of psychoanalysis, was the victim of an uncontrollable addiction to cigars; he smoked about twenty a day. When he was thirty-eight he suffered from arrhythmia (irregular heartbeat) and was told by his physician to stop smoking. He did, for seven weeks. And, in Freud's words, ". . . there were tolerable days. . . . Then came suddenly a severe affection of the heart, worse than I ever had when smoking. . . . And with it an oppression of mood in which images of dying and farewell scenes replaced the more usual fantasies. . . . It is annoying for a doctor who has to be concerned all day long with neurosis, not to know whether he is suffering from a justifiable or hypochondriacal depression."

He had to start smoking again and continued for many years. Once, considerably later, he was able to quit for fourteen months, but even after that time the torture was more than he could bear. Again, he went back to his cigars. He had severe heart reactions, but continued to smoke, although he said it interfered with his studies.

In 1923, when he was sixty-seven, Freud developed cancerous tumors in his palate and jaw. Then began a series of operations — thirty-three in all — that went on for the rest of his life. Later, his heart problems were so severe that he was hospitalized and ordered to give up cigars. He managed to quit smoking, but only for twenty-three days. The operations continued, he eventually lost his jaw, had it replaced with an artificial jaw that caused him constant pain and made it difficult for him to swallow. But he remained addicted to smoking until he died of cancer at age eighty-three.*

Up to a few years ago, no expert in smoking and health would say much more about nicotine than that it was a psychoactive drug, found (in nature) uniquely in tobacco, that it was a powerful alkaloid poison. They agreed that smokers liked it, and wanted it, but the conventional authoritative wisdom was that they didn't really *need* it: that nicotine was not addictive. Therefore, smoking was a habit, in the words of the famous Surgeon General's report, "related primarily to psychological and social drives, reinforced and perpetuated by the pharmacological action of nicotine on the central nervous system, the latter being interpreted subjectively either as stimulant or tranquilizing dependent

---

*Based on an account in *Licit and Illicit Drugs* by Edward Brecher and the editors of Consumer Reports. Boston: Little Brown, 1972.

upon the individual response." Nicotine was *secondary* to smokers' psychology and social behavior. That some smokers found the drug stimulating, and others tranquilizing — known as the "smoker's paradox" — was considered idiosyncratic.

For years, it was accepted that "The tobacco habit should be characterized as an *habituation* rather than an *addiction*," because the Surgeon General's Committee had said so.

Smoking was seen to start in the majority of smokers during adolescence, as experimentation under peer pressure, or revolt against parental authority, which gradually developed into a habit, braided into their lives. The discomfort or distress smokers complained of when they tried to quit, and the many symptoms they reported, ranging from irritability to insomnia, were put down to social or psychological deprivation, nothing more. The Surgeon General's Committee had stated that "No characteristic abstinence syndrome is developed upon withdrawal." The effect of this pronouncement on smokers who, believing in the health hazards reported by the Committee, tried to quit smoking and did feel withdrawal symptoms can be imagined. They were confused and guilt-ridden because they couldn't give up what was only, after all, according to experts merely a habit.

Then, in the 1970s, a number of pharmacologists, psychologists and physicians, funded mainly by the National Institute on Drug Abuse (NIDA), took another look. While agreeing that cigarette smoking has strong emotional ties and social attachments, they were also aware (as noted by the Surgeon General's Committee) that when a great many people smoke a substance habitually — be it opium, marijuana, hashish or cocaine — it's always to get the effect of a pharmacologically active drug. So they began a broad range of studies into nicotine.

Nicotine is one of the deadliest poisons known; 60 mgs (about .002 ounce) can kill an adult human being by paralyzing breathing. Twenty years ago, the average pack of cigarettes delivered this much nicotine in the smoke; the reason smokers didn't drop dead of nicotine poisoning was that they always inhaled nicotine in tiny tokes — seven to ten puffs a cigarette — and the liver quickly metabolized the substance. (Today's average pack delivers a little more than 20 mgs of nicotine, about 1.1 mg per cigarette.) The "half life" of nicotine in the body is only thirty minutes — that is, half of it is metabolized in that time. (It usually takes about eight hours after the last cigarette for all nicotine to leave the body.) Addicted smokers usually have a cigarette every thirty minutes, to replace the nicotine that has been metabolized since their previous smoke.

One thing that had hampered nicotine research was the absence of a test to detect millionths or billionths of a gram of the poison in blood. In the 1970s a group of scientists in Sweden, headed by Dr. Ove Fernö, and another group in London, led by Dr. C. Feyerabend, developed tests sensitive enough to do this; and other tests were created to find nicotine, or its breakdown product (cotanine) in urine, and to measure carbon monoxide in smokers' red blood cells.

After more than five years of experiments in people and animals, many researchers became convinced that nicotine is an addictive drug. While there is no universally accepted definition of addiction, it is known that nicotine meets the criteria of the three sides of the "addictive triad." Smokers develop *tolerance* to nicotine; they become *dependent* on it; and they suffer *withdrawal symptoms* when they don't get it.

Tolerance. A 1978 study showed that smokers could tolerate much higher intravenous doses of nicotine than nonsmokers could — the smokers could handle 700 micrograms (mcgs, or millionths of a gram) without distress compared with only 300 mcgs by nonsmokers. But the nonsmokers quickly developed tolerance: subsequent hourly doses of the drug had progressively less effect on both groups. However, the smokers were always more tolerant of nicotine; they could accept an injection of one milligram (one-thousandth of a gram) of nicotine-base without feeling nausea; in nonsmokers, this dose produced varying degrees of nausea.

Dependence. Harley H. Hanson of the Merck Institute for Therapeutic Research in West Point, Pennsylvania, experimented with six groups of rats. Five got injections of nicotine in different strengths every thirty minutes for forty-eight hours; the sixth group got only saltwater injections. Then the rats were put in cages with food, water, and levers to be pressed. Each time the rats pressed the lever, they were injected with their accustomed dose of nicotine or saltwater.

The rats who had been given nicotine quickly began dosing themselves with increasing frequency, even when the doses were strong enough to cause convulsions. But the rats injected with saltwater pressed their levers hardly at all.

Smokers enjoy nicotine in any form. Some years ago, a researcher gave small doses of the drug hypodermically, intravenously or orally to groups of smokers and nonsmokers. The latter found the effects "queer." But smokers, including the researcher, felt the same as if they'd been smoking, and said that the urge to smoke was greatly reduced when they had a dose of straight nicotine. These experiments were uncontrolled, therefore not considered scientific, but they have been paralleled by other more rigorous work.

For example, a more recent experiment showed that smokers tend to regulate their own doses of nicotine. Fifteen smokers in two groups were given experimental cigarettes containing differing levels of nicotine and tar in a number of variations (low tar/high nicotine, high tar/low nicotine, etc.) Smoking decreased as the delivery of nicotine increased. Variations in the amount of tar had no such effect. According to Ellen R. Gritz of the Laboratory for the Study of Smoking Behavior at the University of California, Los Angeles, evidence from this and other experiments shows that when smokers are given a cigarette lower in nicotine than their accustomed brand, they smoke more cigarettes, and inhale more deeply and/or often, in an effort to keep the nicotine in their blood up to its accustomed level.

The new low-tar cigarettes in the market achieve their single-digit tar and nicotine levels by a number of techniques; the most effective is punching tiny holes in the paper wrapper, above the filter, through which air is drawn into the smoker along with smoke. The low tar/low nicotine effect is therefore mainly one of diluting smoke with air. Many smokers cover these holes, some with their fingers others with tape, thus nullifying the low T/N numbers achieved in the smoking machine. Consciously or unconsciously they achieve their desired dose of nicotine.

Withdrawal.   When smokers first quit smoking, their heart rate slows, their blood pressure rises, brain waves register changes. In heavily addicted smokers, temperature drops; in less-addicted smokers, it rises. All quitters do less well in coordination tests, including driving, than they did when they were smoking. Mouth ulcers are common in quitters. There are sometimes more bizarre effects. In one ex-smoker his voice became extremely hoarse after he quit; another had severe asthma attacks.

The numerous unpleasant, even unbearable symptoms that many smokers suffer when they stop smoking have now been grouped by the American Psychiatric Association's recent manual of mental disorders as the "tobacco withdrawal syndrome." Ex-smokers report, and experiments verify, that their moods swing widely, they are easily irritated and angered, they become more aggressive. The manual also lists under tobacco withdrawal "Anxiety, difficulty in concentrating, restlessness, headache, drowsiness and gastrointestinal disturbances."

"The most important withdrawal symptom is a severe craving for tobacco, reported by about 90 percent of ex-smokers," according to Saul M. Shiffman, psychologist, of the University of South Florida, in Tampa, and Dr. Murray E. Jarvik of UCLA.

From the point of view of nicotine addiction, there are two patterns of smoking. Some smokers smoke only every hour, or less frequently. Analyzing their blood, scientists find peaks and valleys of nicotine. The assumption is that these people are seeking the jolts they get from the drug — for the pleasure or stimulation that these give. But the more addicted smokers smoke at least every half hour. This, as we have seen, is because nicotine begins leaving their bodies in about that length of time. These smokers have a consistently high blood level of nicotine. Dr. Michael A. H. Russell, of the addiction research unit, Maudsley Hospital, London, England, deduces that a steady nicotine level is "the main motive of the addicted heavy smoker" while "optimal peak effects are more important to indulgent smokers who smoke less heavily." In other words, the heavy smoker is seeking to avoid the pain of nicotine withdrawal; while the lighter smoker is doing it more for kicks.

In August 1979, eleven American scientists and physicians met with government experts at the NIDA headquarters in Rockville, Maryland, to study the latest evidence on cigarette smoking. After two days of intensive review, they concluded: "Cigarette smoking is an addiction" and "should be viewed as a disease."

Dr. William Pollin, director of NIDA, said, "Cigarette smoking is a drug dependence, in which a person's freedom of choice has been compromised by the effects of nicotine in the brain and nervous system."

Dr. Russell agrees: "Cigarette smoking is probably the most addictive and dependence-producing form of behavior known to man."

CUTTING DOWN — OR CUTTING OUT?

Shiffman and Jarvik found that smokers who cut down 60 percent on their smoking craved cigarettes as strongly as those who quit "cold turkey." And while the craving soon subsided in those who had stopped smoking, it persisted in those who had only cut down. Nicotine research indicates that the latter are in a constant state of withdrawal.

Some studies do imply that cutting down on smoking may work, if it's done gradually and slowly enough. In a way, all smokers are an example: for all cigarettes now deliver less than half of the tar and nicotine that they put out twenty-five years ago. And according to a government survey, those smokers who continued smoking the same brands (while the T/N content was slowly being diminished without their knowledge) or switched to a brand no more than 25 percent lower than what they had been smoking, did not smoke more cigarettes. This led Daniel Horn, former head of the government agency on smoking and health, to recommend a kind of weaning process, quitting smoking in increments. Horn's theory, based on the survey, was that the body would not feel a 10 percent reduction in nicotine intake. Thus, it might be possible to fool the body's nicotine addiction by changing to a brand of cigarettes no more than 10 percent lower in nicotine and tar. Then, when the smoker became accustomed to the slightly lower T/N brand, he could switch to another brand still 10 percent lower.

Finally, over time, gradually getting to a very low level of nicotine, this theory postulates, it ought to be easy to stop smoking altogether.

In a laboratory situation, a Marlboro smoker was weaned through careful instruction and observation. He was told to reduce the number of puffs per cigarette from his accustomed nine to six. Then he was instructed to make them shorter — he succeeded in cutting them to about half their former duration. Measurements showed he was smoking less tobacco, and that his carbon monoxide intake sharply decreased. So, surprisingly, did his number of cigarettes, from twenty-six to eighteen. After four weeks of this kind of followup, the man spontaneously stopped smoking and was not smoking when tested a year later.

A study by Lawrence Garfinkel of the American Cancer Society does show that smokers of low-nicotine brands are quitting at a rate somewhat faster than that of other smokers. But for most smokers, it seems necessary to quit entirely, in order to stop smoking — cutting down just doesn't work.

NICOTINE'S PARADOXICAL EFFECTS

Initial stimulating effects of nicotine on the cardio-vascular system were described in the chapter "What Happens When You Smoke?" Later effects are contradictory: blood pressure drops, and heart rate slows. Similar antithetical reactions occur throughout the body. The first jolts of nicotine sharpen thinking in both people and animals — they perform memory and learning tasks better. But with continued doses smokers feel tired and let down, even somewhat depressed; their thinking suffers.

The drug has other paradoxical effects. Hitting the brain quickly, at first it galvanizes nerve connections, but continued doses of nicotine block these synapses. It stimulates in the beginning by evoking the discharge of adrenaline and similar energizing catecholamines, then later doses shut them down, producing a more soporific or tranquilizing effect. At first it excites nerves in muscles, but this very quickly turns into an opposite impact, a kind of paralysis. In small doses, nicotine causes tremors; in large doses, convulsions. Small doses increase breathing; large ones slow it down.

Nicotine provokes the vomiting reflex both in the brain and in stomach nerves. It tends to block the flow of urine, while it initially stimulates the intestines — explaining why so many smokers depend on their first cigarette of the day for bowel regularity. Later doses, however, slow down the digestive process. Early doses of nicotine increase the secretion of saliva in the mouth and of mucus in the bronchial tubes; but these effects, too, are reversed with more nicotine.

Since nicotine is now officially identified as the addictive element in cigarettes, it's essential for every smoker who wants to stop to know how badly he or she is addicted to nicotine. The following brief quiz can tell you this about yourself.

Scoring is described after each question:

How Addicted Are You to Nicotine?

(Answer all questions, although some may have been asked in previous quizzes.)

1. How soon after you wake in the morning do you smoke your first cigarette? Score 1 if your answer is within 30 minutes; otherwise 0.

2. Do you find it difficult not to smoke where smoking is forbidden? A "Yes" answer is worth 1; "No" receives 0.

3. Which of all the cigarettes you smoke during the day is the most satisfying? If you say "first cigarette in the morning," you've earned 1 point. Any other answer is 0.

4. How many cigarettes a day do you smoke? 1–15 is a light smoker: score 0. 16–25 cigarettes a day is moderate smoking: 1 point. 25 or more is heavy smoking, give yourself a 2.

5. Do you smoke more during the morning than the rest of the day? "Yes" = 1 point; "No" = 0.

6. Do you smoke when you are sick enough to have to stay in bed? "Yes" = 1 point; "No" = 0.

7. What is the Tar/Nicotine rating of the brand you smoke? To get the value of tar and nicotine in your brand, see the list of Federal Trade Commission smoke assays of U.S. cigarette brands on page 115ff. If your brand is low tar (1–8

mgs)*; score 0. Medium is 9–15 mgs tar; score 1. High is anything above 15 mgs tar, worth 2 points. Note that the nicotine rating is usually about 10 percent of the tar rating; that is, nicotine to tar is usually in the ratio of about 1:10.

8. How often do you inhale? "Occasionally" receives 0 points; "Often" gives you 1 point; "Always" is good for 2 points.

This test was created by Dr. Karl-Olov Fagerström, formerly of the University of Uppsala, Sweden, in 1981.

If you score 0 in the quiz, you are least dependent on cigarettes; a score of 11 indicates maximum dependence. Obviously, a person who doesn't depend much on cigarettes can probably quit smoking rather easily. Until recently, the opposite was also true — but no longer. There is now a good deal of hope and help for the most heavily addicted smokers; they need no longer fear that they are too addicted to stand up to quitting. In fact, the new nicotine chewing gum is actually even more effective in helping nicotine addicts stop smoking than it is with people who smoke only occasionally. Read on.

---

*There is no official standard for low tar. Government agencies call anything under 15 mgs low tar. But researchers sometimes adopt other standards, as in this test.

Step · Three

Stop Smoking

8

Nicotine
Can Help You Quit

SINCE you have read this far, you are a lot closer to quitting than when you started. It is now time for you to know more about the new pharmaceutical product available to help you, and to make it easy for you to stop smoking. It can be had only through your doctor, only on prescription.

More than a decade of experiments with some four thousand smokers by about thirty investigators in a half-dozen countries, tested this product, nicotine chewing gum, and proved the ultimate — and extremely useful — contradiction of nicotine: *this poison which addicts smokers, can be used to break the very addiction it creates. It can, quite literally, help smokers kick their habit. It's most effective with the heaviest smokers; those most addicted to nicotine.*

A tiny dose of nicotine mixed with certain chemicals in a chewing gum base, put up as small square pieces that look like buff-colored Chiclets, and sold under the tradename "Nicorette"* (nicotine resin complex), is the first prescrip-

---

*Nicorette is a registered trademark of Merrell Dow Pharmaceuticals Inc. It is sold in fourteen countries as a prescription drug, and in Switzerland over the counter.

tion drug available in the United States for use in smoking cessation programs. The gum, containing 2 mgs of nicotine, is available in U.S. drugstores. Worldwide, prior to U.S. availability, approximately two million smokers used it to try to give up cigarettes. Estimates are that it helped about 700,000 to stop smoking.

Why give smokers nicotine? Because no other substance has seemed to work. In the judgment of experts, such as the British Royal College of Physicians: "Most people smoke because they are dependent on nicotine." And, according to Dr. Lynn T. Kozlowski of Canada's Addiction Research Foundation in Toronto, Nicorette is the "only pharmaceutical product proved of substantial assistance" to smokers seeking to quit. It is no accident that it is also the only drug product that contains nicotine.

The cigarette habit, perhaps the most tenacious of all drug addictions, incarcerates the smoker in a kind of triangular prison. One wall is cemented to the smoker's environment — made up of work, play, leisure, meals; one wall is an extension of the smoker's inner world, deeply mortared and reinforced by emotions, such as love, hate, joy; *but both are locked into and buttressed by the often irresistible need for nicotine.*

A pack-a-day smoker inhales about 150 to 200 tiny doses of the drug during waking hours. And this goes on every day, day in and day out. No drug-taking habit comes close to this number of fixes. Each dose moves straight from the lungs into the bloodstream and hits the brain in about seven seconds. This is about twice as fast as mainlining heroin (which must first go up the arm, through the right side of the heart, then the lungs and left heart before it reaches the brain).

And nicotine is an extremely powerful drug, with a kick about equal to that of LSD, according to Dr. Reese Jones, professor of psychiatry at the University of California, San Francisco. Both drugs have a threshold level — the level at which a person can feel their effect — of only about one microgram (one millionth of a gram) per kilogram of body weight, when given intravenously.

Nicorette gum can help smokers quit by breaking open the strongest wall of the prison, severing it from the other two. It relieves the smoker from the demands of his chemical addiction by providing smokeless nicotine that is quickly absorbed into the blood via the mucus membrane of the mouth. Thus, smokers can get their drug when they need it without inhaling tar and its cancer-causing chemicals, without breathing in carbon monoxide, thought to be involved in cardiovascular disease, without the irritating gases that are associated with cardiovascular disease and such noncancerous lung diseases as chronic bronchitis and emphysema.

With one wall open to freedom, armored against the initially incessant, often intolerable, symptoms of withdrawal the smoker can more calmly proceed to demolish the social and emotional walls of his or her prison.

Since nicotine is one of the most powerful poisons known how can it be "safe" when packaged in a chewing gum? Because, according to Dr. W. B. Rice of Canada's Health Protection Branch (equivalent of the U.S. Food and Drug Administration), it's in such tiny doses. And, says Dr. Paul Leber of the Psychopharmacological branch of FDA, "A great many medications are powerful poisons: digitalis, cancer drugs for instance. We know about how much nicotine smokers get in smoke; and this product gives less nicotine than a cigarette."

The average cigarette smoker inhales about 1 mg of nicotine in 7.5 minutes. On the other hand, the gum must be chewed slowly, but not steadily, for 30 minutes to extract about 1.8 mgs (90 percent) of its nicotine. Chewers of Nicorette in the 2 mg strength available in the United States have blood levels of the drug generally lower than that of smokers. See graphs on pages 68 and 69. (In other countries, 4 mg gum has also been approved. Chewing it creates blood levels of nicotine approximately equal to the steady levels in smokers.) Because it releases its nicotine slowly, Nicorette does not give the repeated jolts that pleasure smokers seek from cigarettes. It does, however, provide a base level of nicotine, such as that sought by the heaviest, most addicted smokers. In either case, it's just about impossible to overdose by chewing too much Nicorette without first becoming nauseated, a built-in protective factor.

NICORETTE: Nicotine Blood Levels

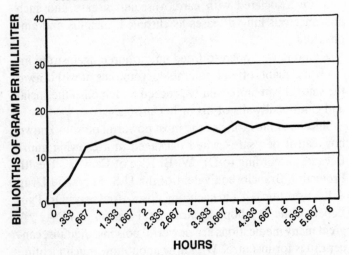

Typical blood level of nicotine in Nicorette user chewing two pieces of 2 mg gum per hour.

McNabb, M. E.; Evert, R. V.; McCusker, K. "Plasma Nicotine Levels Produced by Chewing Nicotine Gum," Journal of the American Medical Association *248 (1982): 865–868.*

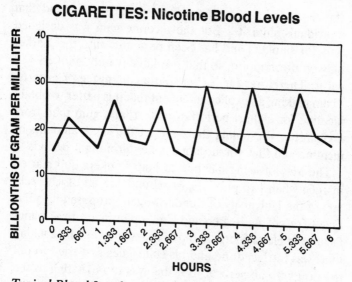

CIGARETTES: Nicotine Blood Levels

Typical Blood Levels of Smoker Smoking One Cigarette Per Hour (1.1 mg nicotine): McNabb, et al. Ibid.

In one safety test, two healthy volunteers were kept off tobacco and nicotine for thirty-six hours, then asked to swallow ten pieces of 4 mg Nicorette. Since swallowed nicotine is largely destroyed by the liver before it reaches the bloodstream, the ten pieces of gum put less nicotine into their bloodstream than smoking a single cigarette. In other tests, while smoking a cigarette lowered skin temperature 2–3 degrees Centigrade, chewing a piece of 2 mg gum had no such effect. Heart rate increased after a cigarette, but not after the 2 mg gum used by normal volunteer subjects. Some rise in blood pressure can occur with the 2 mg nicotine gum as with a cigarette. All in all, chewing a piece of the 2 mg nicotine gum was less toxic than smoking a cigarette.

Dr. Leber notes that nicotine is, indeed, "a toxic substance, and that most physicians would recommend that individuals shun it." But the nicotine gum was designed only for smokers and has been permitted into the market only on prescription, so that presumably only smokers will get it. Therefore, Dr. Leber told a committee of experts, "I am making an explicit judgment that it is better to obtain nicotine for a short period of time from a gum than from a cigarette. Presuming that you get the same amounts of nicotine and that you do not smoke during that period."

The idea of using nicotine to help smokers quit started in 1969 when two physiologists (Lundgren and Lichtneckert) of the University of Lund, Sweden, proposed it to Dr. Ove Fernö of A. B. Leo and Co., a pharmaceutical manufacturer in Helsingborg. Fernö, a heavy smoker who couldn't quit, was intrigued; he and his colleagues first tried to put the drug into an aerosol. But this was too irritating to the nose. A liquid form, given by mouth, was destroyed in the digestive system. The only practical solution that would minimize the chance of accidental poisoning was a chewing gum. After a couple of years of experiments, they worked out a system of binding nicotine into a chewing gum with an "ion exchange resin," which gives up nicotine at a slow rate when it comes into contact with saliva as it is chewed.

Early experiments with smokers were not encouraging. The reason, Fernö found, was that the nicotine would penetrate the mucus membrane of the mouth only in an alkaline environment. That is, making the mouth alkaline permits nicotine to enter the bloodstream directly from the oral cavity. (This is the reason why cigar smokers need not inhale to get their satisfaction. Cigar smoke is alkaline, and the nicotine is absorbed in the mouth. Thus, cigar smokers have much less lung cancer than cigarette smokers, who are forced to inhale their smoke — because it's acid — to extract nicotine.) Fernö knew that if he added "buffers" —

antacids such as sodium bicarbonate — to the gum, the nicotine could be absorbed as it was released. At last he had found a delivery system for nicotine that did not require inhaling it. Experimentally, the new formula began producing astounding results.

In 1975, a British magazine editor met Dr. Michael A. H. Russell. The fifty-year-old editor was inhaling the smoke of a great many pipes and cigarettes, and was very anxious to quit. He had been able to give up his habit about three or four times, for brief periods, but inevitably relapsed. Dr. Russell told him about Nicorette, which he was testing in his quit-smoking programs. The editor enrolled in the very strict protocol, which started with his being forced to acknowledge that he was a smoking addict, and which included chewing one piece of 4 mg gum at precisely every hour twelve times a day, and keeping a careful record of every smoke. He had to report weekly. After about three weeks on the gum, the editor found that he had greatly reduced his smoking. And at twelve weeks his notebook showed he was smoking so little that Russell suggested he quit. It was "the most painless thing I've ever done," he said. After a few weeks, his gum was switched to the 2 mg strength; he continued chewing until his supply ran out and then stopped. He hasn't chewed Nicorette or smoked for nine years.

Dr. Russell, perhaps the world's leading authority on nicotine addiction, has been researching intensive quit-smoking methods since 1969. "We have tried electric-aversion therapy [electric shock with each cigarette] rapid smoking [tends to produce nausea], covert sensitization and Q-exposure, and had only about 15 to 25 percent not smoking after one year, not always chemically validated.* Nicorette

---

*Smokers are not reliable witnesses about quitting their habit. Sound research always checks their blood, urine or saliva for signs of smoking — that is, for nicotine, cotanine, thiocyanate, or carbon monoxide.

changed all this; it has doubled the success rate, and we believe that it is a geniune breakthrough in the treatment of smoking cessation after years of frustration." In one study, Russell recruited 116 smokers, and assigned them to twelve quit-smoking groups, meeting weekly with a psychiatrist or psychologist. Each group was given at random 2 mg Nicorette or a placebo gum that looked and tasted like Nicorette (it contained 1 mg of nicotine, unbuffered, so it was not absorbed and had no pharmacological effect). The therapists and patients were "blind" — none knew who had the nicotine, or the inactive gum. All patients were told to stop smoking over three days, and to chew as often as they wished.

At one month, 24 percent of the placebo and 48 percent of the Nicorette group were not smoking (verified by blood tests). When followed up at one year, the differences were even more striking: only 14 percent in the placebo group were still not smoking, as against 31 percent who were verified quitters in the Nicorette group.

In a number of experiments in several countries, other things being equal, using the gum increased the quit rate of smokers by 50 to 100 percent. But every expert interviewed for this report tempered his enthusiasm for the product with caution: it is no panacea that will magically make all smokers quit. Rather, it is a powerful ally to programs that aid and support the smoker during the quitting process. Those that give the most intensive support, like Russell's, and attract the smokers most motivated to quit, have the highest rate of success. However, even the best programs using Nicorette achieve only about 50 percent success at the end of a one year followup.

Dr. Leber and others see Nicorette as a parallel to methadone, used in intensive programs to wean heroin addicts from their drug. However, unlike methadone, which is itself addictive, discontinuation of Nicorette use has not been a problem.

A Canadian physician, head of family medicine at a Canadian university, consumes forty cigarettes a day. Since smoking is almost an aberration among doctors, he has often tried to quit. When he did, he was "climbing the walls," says his friend Dr. Walter Rosser, head of family medicine at the University of Ottowa. "We gave him Nicorette, and he was able to stop smoking, something he'd never been able to do. But only for six months. Then he said that his jaws hurt from chewing so much gum. He began smoking again."

Soreness of the temporomandibular joint — where the lower and upper jaws are connected — was a problem with some heavy Nicorette users, but no more so than with chewing any other gum. In a study of the effects of the gum on mouth tissues at Indiana University School of Dentistry, mouth ulcers in Nicorette chewers were no different from those found among people who have quit smoking — it's a common result of quitting. In this study 208 smokers were given either Nicorette or a placebo gum at random. At six weeks, 70 percent of both groups were still chewing gum, averaging about seven or eight pieces a day. There was one dramatic difference: 34.3 percent of the Nicorette group had quit smoking versus only 10.7 percent of the placebo chewers. Yet, principal investigator Dr. Arden Christen found no more irritation of the gums in the Nicorette group than the other — but all subjects who continued to smoke had more gingivitis than those who quit. In fact, among Nicorette users who quit cigarettes, there was less plaque and calculus (calcified deposits on teeth) than among smokers; similarly, stained teeth seemed confined to smokers, no matter which gum they chewed.

One of the most interesting findings of the Indiana study

was that smokers most addicted on nicotine — determined by a special questionnaire — were more likely to quit with Nicorette. Their quit rate after one month was 46 percent, as against only 29 percent among less nicotine-dependent smokers.

In fact, the indications are that the smokers most addicted to nicotine are most likely to benefit from Nicorette. Such smokers are those who use more than fifteen cigarettes a day, prefer brands with more than 0.9 mgs nicotine, usually inhale, smoke the first cigarette within thirty minutes of arising, find that one hardest to give up, smoke more frequently in the morning than later, find it difficult not to smoke in "no smoking" areas and smoke even if they're forced to stay in bed because of illness.

Even to smokers, nicotine is often unpleasant. Thus, in the Christen and Russell studies, there were significantly more hiccups and nausea in Nicorette users than in those chewing placebo gum. Among Russell's subjects, twice as many Nicorette users had indigestion or felt sick as those on placebo.

On October 24, 1983, the forty-year-old assistant managing editor of a San Antonio, Texas, newspaper visited Dr. Harry A. Croft, a psychiatrist who was helping his teenage son through leukemia therapy. Because of the emotional strain of his son's cancer, the editor was smoking four to five packs of cigarettes a day. He saw a sign in Dr. Croft's office: "A New Way to Quit Smoking." Asking about it, he got a short lecture on quitting and a supply of Nicorette. He pitched his cigarettes and lighter into the doctor's wastebasket, and hasn't smoked since. At first he chewed as many as sixteen gums a day, later this dropped to about five or six. When interviewed, he said he expected to give up the gum soon, but would probably carry a supply around with him, just in case.

When Nicorette was approved as a prescription drug in

Great Britain, Russell did a study of 1938 cigarette-smoking patients of thirty-four general practitioners. Of patients who received only advice to quit smoking, and an instruction booklet, 4.1 percent were not smoking after one year; but those who were also given Nicorette did more than twice as well: 8.8 percent were still off cigarettes after a year. And in a small subgroup of patients who asked for and used more than one box of chewing gum, 24 percent were abstinent. If this experience holds good for physicians and patients here, U.S. general practitioners and internists might help some six million American smokers to kick their habit each year. Since, according to the Royal College of Physicians, "between 2.5 and 4 of each 10 smokers will die because of their smoking," this might save many of those six million Americans from premature death.

Experiments show that the gum is most effective if used for three months. Studies show that people who stop smoking with the gum and then stop the gum too soon are more likely to relapse. And many therapists recommend that their patients carry a supply with them indefinitely — not to use, necessarily, but as a security blanket if they get the impulse to smoke. The FDA does not recommend use beyond six months.

In the United States, Nicorette is available in the 2 mg strength, in blister packages which are child resistant. A box of ninety-six pieces, about an average ten days' supply, costs $20 — about fifty cents a day more than the average smoker (thirty cigarettes) spends on smoking. But unlike cigarettes Nicorette gets cheaper as the ex-smoker tapers down on chewing. All in all, a smoker ought to be able to kick a habit that costs about $550 a year, for an investment of perhaps $150 to $200 in chewing gum, plus whatever help is needed in support services.

9

When, Where
and How to Quit

*T*HE most important step you must now take is to *decide* to quit. You've been thinking about it, reading about it, learning about it — now, *DO IT!*

Call your doctor and tell him/her that you want help. Perhaps you've tried this in the past without much success. Although more doctors have quit smoking than any other group, until recently few actively encouraged their patients to do so. The reason: they had nothing to offer but advice.

But now doctors can write a prescription for something effective: nicotine chewing gum.

It should be noted that you may be able to quit without Nicorette (nicotine resin complex). Millions of people did so during the years before it became available. Merely following the steps in this book can help you stop smoking. But using the gum gives you a much better chance of succeeding. In careful trials, no matter what sort of quit smoking method was used, adding Nicorette to the program increased the success rate by from 50 to 100 percent.

Ask your physician about it. He or she may want to know more about the gum before giving you a prescription, or may have several patients like you who want to quit.

Let's suppose you've got your prescription for Nicorette, and had it filled. What do you do next? Now, today, choose a time or date to stop smoking. Apply what you've learned from this book to make it easiest for yourself, especially the tests you've taken. Here's how:

If you're a pleasure smoker it's going to be simplest for you to quit if you occupy your time and avoid for a month the pleasurable situations in your life linked with smoking.

If you're a stress smoker, it will facilitate your quitting if you stop smoking during a tranquil period — an ideal time is a holiday, or vacation.

After you've picked a date, make a public commitment: tell your family, friends and co-workers that you're stopping smoking. If they smile, so much the better — it'll challenge you. And even if they don't, your pride won't let you go back on your promise to so many people.

The next move is simple: Start chewing Nicorette, and stop smoking completely, entirely and all at once. It's as simple as that. This is not the same as going cold turkey because the gum will carry you over the withdrawal symptoms. Thus, quitting will not be as difficult as you imagined, or perhaps experienced in a previous attempt. It's hard to believe, but the gum takes the sting and apprehension out of stopping — by avoiding, or at least greatly mitigating, the craving for a smoke and other post-smoking symptoms that caused so many to relapse in the past.

One thing is virtually certain: gradually cutting down on cigarettes doesn't work for most people. In some early experiments, patients were permitted both to chew Nicorette and smoke for a while, before they finally gave up cigarettes. But the evidence in thousands of people proves that the easiest way to quit is to stop smoking. Cutting down, it's been found, feeds the habit just enough to put the smoker into a steady state of withdrawal. It almost guarantees re-lapse.

Before you try Nicorette, you have to know how it works and how to use it. Read the following:

In an ideal world, every patient who gets a prescription for Nicorette will also receive printed instructions on how to use it. These have been carefully worked out by the manufacturer with the Food and Drug Administration, based on the experience of patients in clinical trials. Their purpose: to see that patients get the most out of the gum, and to avoid side effects as much as possible. However, in the real world, many patients will not get the FDA-approved instructions, or may ignore them. The following is based on patient information on Nicorette which accompanies the product. These instructions summarize the important facts about Nicorette; they do not cover all information about the drug. If you have questions not answered here, consult your physician.

How to Use the Gum

Whenever you feel the urge to smoke, put one piece in your mouth. Chew it slowly until you taste it — it has a somewhat peppery taste, not unpleasant, but not like regular chewing gum — or until you feel a tingling sensation in your mouth. As you chew, nicotine is being released slowly along with antacids that permit it to be absorbed through the lining of your mouth. You will get the taste or the tingling sensation usually after about fifteen chews — the number is not the same for all people. As soon as you get the taste of the gum, or the tingling sensation in your mouth, stop chewing. But keep the Nicorette in your mouth — park it between cheek and gum. The gum is sugarless, hence not likely to cause cavities.

After the taste or tingling is about gone (about one minute later) chew *slowly* again until you taste the gum. Then stop chewing again.

Remember, this is not ordinary chewing gum. The reason for the slow chewing and stopping and starting is to get the maximum amount of nicotine at a rate at which you can most comfortably absorb it without becoming sick. If you follow these instructions, you will get the optimum benefit from one piece of gum in about thirty minutes of stop-and-start slow chewing.

Do not expect the gum to give you the same quick satisfaction that smoking does. As noted in the previous chapter, it will provide you with a steady blood level of nicotine, not the jolts you get from smoking. The purpose is to control the withdrawal symptoms that you may have experienced in a previous attempt to quit cigarettes — or which you've heard so much about, you were fearful of trying.

Most people find that ten to twelve pieces of 2 mg Nicorette per day are enough to control their urge to smoke. It is unlikely that you will need even this much — but, in any case, do not chew more than thirty pieces of Nicorette in any one day. (That's a huge amount; since one piece lasts for thirty minutes, you would be chewing for fifteen hours a day.)

Depending on your needs, you can adjust the rate of chewing and the time between pieces.

If you chew the gum too fast, you may get effects like those you had when you inhaled a cigarette for the first time, or when you smoke too fast. These include light-headedness, nausea and vomiting, throat and mouth irritation, hiccups and stomach upset. Most such effects are usually controlled by chewing more slowly. Some others sometimes seen — particularly during the first few days of using the gum — include mouth ulcers, jaw muscle ache, headache, heart palpitations and more than the usual amount of saliva in the mouth. These are common, but not inevitable. Most people who use Nicorette do not experience most of these side effects. They, too, are usually controlled by slower chewing.

Nicorette has been formulated to minimize stickiness. As with other gums, however, the degree to which Nicorette may stick to your dentures, dental caps or partial bridges may depend on the materials from which they are made and other factors. Should an excessive degree of stickiness to your dental work occur, there is the possibility that, as with other gums, Nicorette may damage dental work, and you should discontinue its use and consult your physician or dentist.

If you accidentally swallow a piece of gum you will probably feel no effects, as almost none of its nicotine will be absorbed in the stomach or intestines. However, if you do have any unpleasant reactions after swallowing a piece of gum, call your doctor. Overdosage could occur if many pieces are chewed simultaneously or in rapid succession. However, too much nicotine is likely to make you sick before reaching a dangerous level. In case of overdose, call your doctor or local poison center.

As your urge to smoke fades, gradually reduce the number of pieces of gum you chew each day. This may be possible within two to three months. However, unless your physician tells you otherwise, *do not attempt to stop using the gum until your CRAVING IS SATISFIED with one or two pieces a day.*

Even though you may have quit smoking weeks or months before, remember to carry the gum with you at all times in case you feel the sudden urge to smoke. Do not forget that in ex-smokers one cigarette may start the smoking habit again.

Six months on Nicorette should be more than enough time to rid yourself of both smoking and the craving to start. After that length of time, you should stop using Nicorette.

Some warnings and reminders: Don't use Nicorette if you are pregnant. It contains nicotine, which may cause harm to the fetus. And, of course, don't smoke, either; smoking, which takes in carbon monoxide and tar as well as nicotine, is even worse for the fetus than nicotine alone.

If you are a nursing mother, Nicorette is contraindicated, because nicotine will be transmitted through your milk, and your baby will swallow it.

It's important to avoid pregnancy while using Nicorette. But if you do suspect that you may be pregnant, stop using the gum immediately and see your doctor at once.

Remember, this drug has been prescribed for you. Please don't let anyone else use it. And, like all other medications, make sure it's out of the reach of children.

If a child chews or swallows one or more pieces of the gum, you should contact your physician or local poison control center immediately. Nicotine poisoning is not uncommon in our society because nicotine is used in many insecticides; doctors and poison specialists know how to handle the problem.

Since Nicorette is not a panacea, don't expect it to make you stop smoking merely because you've started chewing. It was not designed to work alone. It will help you stop, it will make it easy to stop, and it will help you stay off cigarettes — but for maximum effectiveness, use as many stratagems, tricks and gimmicks as you can think of to help your cause. Anything that is legal, moral and nonfattening is okay.

Should you try acupuncture, hypnosis, group therapy, a quit-smoking clinic? None of these can hurt, any may help, depending on your own needs, wants and attitudes. However, Dr. Donald T. Frederickson, an expert in this field, says, "I believe only a small percentage of smokers will ultimately require professional support. Most individuals are perfectly capable of stopping smoking on their own once they've made a *decision* to stop."

The fact is, about 95 percent of people who stop smoking do so on their own.

Here are some tips that may help:

• With your doctor's approval, you may want to step up physical activity. Walking more, for example. Or swimming. Don't suddenly go in for violent exercise such as tennis or jogging if you've been leading a sedentary life. You need the guidance of an expert in physical education or sports medicine to ease yourself into such activities.

• Avoid places, people, occasions and activities you have associated with smoking, as much as possible. As an example, if you're used to smoking after coffee, it might be a good idea to switch to tea for a while.

• Make your own "Smoker's Survival Kit," including Nicorette, flavored toothpicks, a plastic straw, things to chew on. Remember, smoking is, in part, something you do with your hands and mouth. If you keep your mouth busy with chewing, or sucking on a straw, you're less likely to need the oral gratification of a cigarette. Drink lots of water, fruit juices and low-calorie soft drinks — anything that keeps your hands and mouth busy when you want a cigarette.

• When you are tensed up and want to relax with a cigarette, try this instead: Sit down. Let yourself go completely limp — neck, arms, legs. Then take the deepest possible breath, inhaling slowly and fully. Then hold your breath, count to five, and just as slowly exhale.

• Visit a friend — a *nonsmoking* friend. Knit. Get some worry beads and keep them in your pocket. Take them out when you feel the itch to reach for a cigarette.

• Try the buddy system — many people find it easier to quit if they can share the experience, compare notes, be able to telephone the friend in a time of crisis or triumph. Perhaps your buddy can be someone who has quit and understands your problem. Or someone like yourself, who is trying to quit and wants a bit of encouragement or support from time to time.

Step · Four

Quit Smoking—
Permanently

What Happens
When You Quit Smoking
— and Why

DIAGNOSTIC CRITERIA FOR TOBACCO WITHDRAWAL

A. Use of tobacco for at least several weeks at a level equivalent to more than ten cigarettes per day, with each cigarette containing at least 0.5 mg of nicotine.

B. Abrupt cessation of or reduction in tobacco use, followed within 24 hours by at least four of the following:

1) craving for tobacco
2) irritability
3) anxiety
4) difficulty in concentrating
5) restlessness
6) headache
7) drowsiness
8) gastrointestinal disturbances

— *Diagnostic and Statistical Manual of Mental Disorders.* Third Edition. *American Psychiatric Association*

W HAT most smokers didn't know about the effects of quitting on their bodies, minds and feelings prevented some from trying to quit (fearing the withdrawal symptoms would be unbearable) and drove others to begin smoking again.

Since these symptoms are largely related to nicotine withdrawal, when you quit smoking you need not fear them so long as nicotine chewing gum is available. However, it's always less threatening to know what to expect, even if you have the weapon to counteract it.

A number of new, previously unreported scientific studies explain the often bewildering (to the ex-smoker) effects of giving up cigarettes, tell you how long these may last, and offer successful strategies for dealing with the urge to start smoking again.

DO YOU HAVE TO GAIN WEIGHT WHEN YOU STOP SMOKING?

One of the factors that prevents many smokers, particularly women, from attempting to quit, is the fear of gaining weight. People who smoke cigarettes weigh less, on the average, than nonsmokers of the same age. Must they become obese when they quit? If so, why — and can they control this?

There have been three theoretical explanations about weight gain after quitting smoking: that ex-smokers increase their food intake to replace the oral gratification of smoking; that stopping smoking lowers their metabolism; that quitters tend to eat more high-calorie foods.

Dr. Neil Grunberg of the Uniformed Services University of the Health Sciences in Maryland has done animal and human studies that give important clues to the answer.

Dr. Grunberg began with rats that had been addicted to nicotine via injections of that substance, and a control group of animals that had received only saline injections. Given equal access to the same foods, when the nicotine-habituated rats were deprived of their drug they began to eat more and gain abnormal amounts of weight. More significantly, they sought the sweetest-tasting foods. When they were given nicotine again, their taste preference shifted back to the lower-calorie, least-sweet-tasting foods. Rats on saline solution ate a normal diet and gained weight more slowly, but steadily, a characteristic of the species given an unlimited food supply.

Grunberg repeated this experiment in people. He persuaded groups of cigarette smokers and nonsmokers to join an experiment ostensibly to test their taste threshold. They could choose snacks from any of three groups of foods. One was made up of chocolate bars, gumdrops, and jellybeans; another offered salted crackers, pretzels and salami; the third consisted of unsalted crackers and peanuts, and a very bland cheese. He permitted half the smokers to smoke whenever they wished; and asked the other half not to smoke for twelve hours (to make sure that nicotine would have disappeared from their bodies). Smokers, temporary abstainers and nonsmokers could eat as much as they wished of anything they wanted.

The people duplicated rat behavior: smokers who had quit for twelve hours ate like rats deprived of nicotine: they invariably selected the sweetest foods; steady smokers chose the blandest, lowest calorie fare; nonsmokers ate a variety from all groups.

Dr. Grunberg also analyzed the food consumption of the United States population during the years 1969–1972. The reason: during those years, there had been a large dip in per capita smoking in this country. About ten million more people gave up cigarettes during these years than the number who normally would have quit through attrition (those who give up smoking had usually been older smokers who developed smoking-related disease symptoms and stopped for health reasons). The generally accepted explanation for this upsurge in quitting is that this was the period when the Federal Communications Commission forced broadcasters, under the "fairness doctrine," to run thousands of anti-smoking spots on radio and TV (in a ratio of one to every four paid cigarette commercials).

During this great move away from smoking, the U.S. rate of sugar consumption (adjusted for price changes) went up about as fast as cigarette smoking went down.

Aware of ex-smokers' need to replace nicotine with sugar, Dr. Ellen Gritz of UCLA advises her patients who quit smoking to stick to low-calorie foods. None who followed her instructions has ever had a weight problem.

Not all ex-smokers gain weight. But many do, and it isn't always just a few pounds. This is unsettling, and perhaps costly — normal wardrobes don't fit, new clothes have to be bought. This factor affects many people's decision to quit, or to start smoking again. But purely from the point of view of health, even a substantial weight gain is a worthwhile tradeoff for giving up smoking. In order to equal the risks of smoking a pack a day, the former smoker would have to become eighty to ninety pounds overweight.

Careful management under a physician's care can help you avoid the weight gain. And you may be able to help yourself stay at your regular clothes size with these gambits:

• Make a conscious effort to note the additional food, and the richer foods, you may be eating as a result of quitting smoking.

• Keep a food diary, and note every time you eat or drink something.

• Buy a paperback calorie counter and figure out how many more calories you're eating.

• Eat small snacks, more frequently — five or six times a day, rather than three heavy meals. It is healthier in general to eat smaller amounts more frequently than the usual "three squares."

- Refuse second helpings.
- Watch your weight by weighing yourself daily.
- Eat low-calorie foods, avoid rich desserts (eat fruit instead), stop using butter and margarine, take a noncaloric sweetener in your coffee, drink sugar-free soft drinks, have a glass of wine rather than a cocktail, and don't drink beer.

Smoking cigarettes creates a dependence that is perhaps stronger than that of other drugs. One study showed that cigarette smokers and heroin addicts quit at about the same rate — and relapsed at the same rates, as well.

Because tobacco does create drug tolerance and dependence, when smokers stop using it they suffer withdrawal symptoms, like other drug addicts. Karl-Olov Fagerström documented the major physiological effects of smoking and cessation.

First Fagerström checked the smokers' levels of addiction with the test you've taken on page 61 ("How Addicted Are You?"). He found that the best predictor of addiction was the time when smokers took their first cigarette of the day. Those who lit up first thing in the morning, before their feet hit the floor, and chain-smoked their first two or three cigarettes, were the most heavily addicted and would experience the severest physical withdrawal effects.

Body Temperature. Fagerström checked body temperature of twenty-six smokers in a quit-smoking clinic two weeks before, and two days after, they quit using cigarettes. He found that in the lightest, least-addicted smokers, body temperature went up when they stopped; in heavily addicted smokers, it dropped.

The Swedish researcher also found a strange phenomenon in ex-smokers. He asked fifteen of them who hadn't smoked for at least six months to smoke a single cigarette. *Their heart rate increased in inverse proportion to their former level*

of addiction: the most addicted had the least change in pulse.
This appears to indicate that the tolerance for nicotine,
unlike that for hard drugs, does not diminish with time. In
fact, there are indications that it may last a lifetime — one
reason, perhaps, why ex-smokers who had been addicted
to nicotine cannot risk smoking even a single cigarette again.

Heart Rate. It's been documented that heart rate increases in anyone who smokes a single cigarette. Fagerström
measured this in nineteen regular smokers while each puffed
for fifteen seconds, inhaling approximately equal volumes
of smoke. Heart rates went up from three to thirty-three
beats per minute. Lowest increases were in the heaviest,
most addicted smokers (e.g., those with the highest tolerance for nicotine).

Tolerance. In animal experiments, those addicted to morphine lose their tolerance and dependence steadily after the
drug is withdrawn. When it's given to them months later,
they react as though they'd never had it before. In nicotine-
addicted animals, however, months after withdrawal a dose
of the drug produces the same reactions as when the animals
were getting their regular doses, further evidence of long-
term nicotine tolerance.

Sleep Disturbances. Some effects of quitting smoking are
paradoxical, like nicotine's. We have seen that the drug
may be both stimulating and tranquilizing. This may explain
why ex-smokers suffer two different kinds of sleep disturbances. Their daytime "slow brain waves" (measured by an
electroencephalograph) increase, indicating drowsiness —
a common complaint of quitters. But during the night, these
same people suffer from insomnia. While awake, they seem
to miss nicotine's kick; at night, they need its tranquilizing
effect.

Digestive Changes. Anyone who smokes tobacco for the first time has a visceral reaction: the desire to throw up. But as smokers develop tolerance for the drug, they lose this impulse.

The day's first dose of nicotine in the smoker stimulates the large intestine. Thus, as noted earlier, many smokers use cigarettes as a bowel regulator.

As the day wears on, repeated doses of nicotine slow down digestion, one way that the drug diminishes appetite. It also stimulates the flow of saliva, an important factor in appetite and digestion.

Being addicted to a drug with such varied and contradictory intestinal effects may explain the bizarre and often contradictory changes in digestion experienced by many ex-smokers: nausea, constipation, diarrhea.

Craving. The most frequent and severe symptom of tobacco withdrawal is craving for tobacco, says psychologist Saul Shiffman of the University of South Florida. This afflicts at least 90 percent of former smokers, generally reaches its peak within the first twenty-four hours after stopping, and tapers down over the next seven days. Then it starts rising and persists for four to eight weeks in most ex-smokers. In fact, it has been seen to recur occasionally as long as five years after quitting.

Shiffman, an expert in smoking relapse, says that craving for smoke is the single most compelling factor that drives ex-smokers back to their habit. But awareness of this overpowering drive can to some extent help to resist it. Studies reveal that craving is repetitive but temporary, it usually lasts in its most intense form for only three to five minutes. And it follows a predictable daily pattern; it's least insistent in the morning, and rises during the day to reach its peak in the evening. And it disappears more quickly from smokers who quit entirely, than those who attempt to taper down.

The latter suffer most: craving becomes a tenacious monkey glued to their backs; they're feeding their habit just enough to whet its appetite.

Withdrawal symptoms are not necessarily overpowering — and need not occur in all smokers who quit but, as might be expected, they're strongest and most frequent in the heaviest smokers: those who burn more than thirty cigarettes a day, estimated to be a majority of our smoking population. When they quit, "Changes in mood and performance can be detected within two hours of the last cigarette," according to the *Psychiatric Manual*. But that was before Nicorette was available to counteract the physical addiction.

How to Stay Off Cigarettes for the Rest of Your Life

I read an article about how poor people suffered in India. I tried to picture my own children in this same plight, and thought how wonderful it would be if someone would give us enough money so they wouldn't have to go to bed hungry. So I began putting aside the money I would have spent on smoking and after two months turned it over to CARE; I still donate my "cigarette money" to useful causes.

When I quit smoking, there was a kind of empty feeling in my chest. I could soothe this with a sort of vegetable cocktail. Recipe: a quart of tomato juice, ³/₄ cup of lemon juice, Tabasco sauce, Worcestershire sauce, salt and pepper to taste. The tangier the better.

When I went about my business without a cigarette, I would be tempted to buy a pack. But if I carried one cigarette, it gave me a sense of security. Then I didn't panic; I could smoke if I had to — so I didn't have to. [Note: this person quit smoking before Nicorette was available. Instead of a cigarette, carry a package of the gum as a security blanket.]

One smoker had a case of influenza that lasted for four weeks, during which she had no desire to smoke, it just tasted too bad. After that length of time, she said to herself, the habit is broken, why start again? Instead, she began putting aside the money she would have spent;

*in a year she had a tidy sum. With it, a stockbroker
friend bought her 20 shares of stock — which went up
about 100 points. She sold out, and put the money into
a bluechip stock that brings her a regular income —
from not smoking.*

   *When you want to smoke, take a shower — ever tried
to smoke in a shower?*

   — FIVE PERSONAL STRATEGIES FOR STAYING
   OFF CIGARETTES

*I*N the previous chapter, we dealt with the physiological
symptoms of withdrawal, caused by the absence of nicotine.
However, no drug addiction is entirely chemical: all have
emotional and psychological and social aspects. What helps
make cigarette smoking probably the most addictive form
of drug taking is that it is more rooted in every aspect of
its addicts' lives. For while other addictive drugs are illicit,
therefore expensive — often carrying criminal penalties —
may be difficult to find, and are acceptable usually only
among other users, tobacco cigarettes are legal, they're relatively cheap, and can be smoked just about anywhere,
except in proscribed public places.

   Thus, quitting cigarettes not only interrupts the flow of
a drug tolerated and demanded by the brain and nervous
system, the heart, circulation and digestion, but tears out
a habit that is socially oriented.

   For you, as for other smokers, quitting also means dis-
secting out of your waking hours a behavior that has been
rooted for years or decades. You must change your accustomed self-image from that of a smoker to that of a nonsmoker. Creating a new persona, a fresh concept of oneself,
and filling the voids left by an old habit, take time and

effort. But it is now much easier, since the physical withdrawal can be blunted with Nicorette, leaving you free to deal with the emotional psychosocial parts of the habit in a calm and organized way.

Dr. Saul Shiffman is the author of a unique study of the successes and failures of 183 men and women who quit smoking. From their hard-won experience, Shiffman has learned what made quitters backslide, when and where they encountered the most problems, what their most difficult problems were, and how successful quitters handled these situations without getting hooked again. His subjects were graduates of smoking clinics who hadn't smoked for at least three days. His "laboratory" was a telephone hot-line that these people could call at any time of the day or night when they felt the urge to smoke, or had actually done so.

Shiffman learned that smoking relapse didn't just happen but invariably followed a "relapse crisis" — a threat to abstinence. Whether the ex-smoker dealt with the crisis successfully or not, all felt a sense of guilt and failure — for, having stopped smoking, they expected no further problems. And their sense of failure was one of the main causes of relapse.

The crisis always occurred "at the intersection of a triggering situation and a deficient coping response." What this means is that craving for tobacco had to occur under specific circumstances, and at a specific time and place; the ex-smoker's ability to anticipate, recognize, and deal with these events predicted whether he/she would succumb or not: this is what is meant by coping.

The most dangerous moments were when the ex-smoker had been eating, or drinking alcohol, with people who were smoking and where cigarettes were easily available. Next most threatening periods were when the former smoker was relaxing at home, after dinner. Third on the list of hazardous situations was usually at work, when the quitter felt pressured or frustrated. Another risky time was at home during periods of boredom or depression.

"Relapse prevention," says Shiffman, "depends on preparing ex-smokers to cope with these high-risk situations." There are four basic successful strategies:

Avoidance. A number of touchy situations can be anticipated, and avoided. For example, during the first few weeks after quitting, stay away from parties. Don't let yourself be trapped in long waiting periods of unstructured time. The temptation is to fill the void with smoke: one successful ex-smoker always carried a paperback book, another a crossword puzzle, to occupy themselves if such occasions arose.

Sitting at table after a meal creates a strong temptation to smoke because that's when cigarettes tasted best. A useful strategy is simply to get up and go into another room for coffee, or clear the table immediately after eating, or just take a walk.

But what can you do if trouble can't be avoided?

Escape. If possible take a break from a stressful meeting, for example; move away from smokers at a party that you can't avoid attending, excuse yourself from taking a cocktail. Since craving comes in short bursts, escaping from the triggering situation for just a few minutes can prevent relapse. And, of course, you've always got your nicotine chewing gum, not magic, but very supportive if you use it as often as you need it.

Distraction. Craving may come on when you have no chance to escape — driving a car, say, waiting in line, meeting with colleagues. One ex-smoker successfully distracted herself from craving while driving or waiting at the checkout counter by simply humming to herself. Other distractions are concentrating on something pleasant, like an upcoming vacation, or imagining a favorite spot or sport. Switching behaviors — a trip to the watercooler, vacuuming the apartment, mending a broken chair — are also successful distractions from the urge to smoke.

Delay. Another solution is simply to grit one's teeth and wait the craving out — knowing it isn't going to last forever. Telling yourself, "I'll wait five minutes while chewing my Nicorette and then decide if I can't bear it" can bridge the time; "I'll just finish what I'm doing and see how I feel then" can hurdle the pressure to smoke. "It's easier to say 'no' for a few minutes than forever," Shiffman notes — and by the time the few minutes have elapsed, the urge will likely have abated.

These general strategies are a first line of defense against relapse. But as an ex-smoker you need defense in depth, as well.

Negative emotions — frustration, worry, anxiety, embarrassment, anger and depression — are most likely to trigger smoking. Quitters who cope successfully with these feelings use several techniques:

Self-talk. Some people find it supportive to conjure up images of blackened, withered lungs — the result of smoking; or a sore throat; or the notion that smoking will make them feel ill, perhaps put them in the hospital. (It might be a good idea to go back and look at the chapter on "What Happens When You Smoke" and the chart on the "Dangers of Smoking, and the Benefits of Quitting.") Others do better summoning up positive images of themselves in which by not smoking they are healthy, active, breathing easily and enjoying the company (and approval) of nonsmoking friends and family. Or they may plan how they're going to spend the $550 (tax free) they'll save in a year of not smoking thirty cigarettes a day.

Another kind of self-talk is an interior dialogue, first identifying the source of stress and then asking yourself, "What's going on here, what do I really want out of this?" Trying for an optimistic view — "This isn't so bad, it could be worse" — or concentrating on a pleasant outcome of present stress are other techniques that work. Instead of tensing up while waiting for a friend who's late, view the time as an opportunity to relax. A simple technique is to take a few deep breaths, and visualize your muscles going limp, starting with your toes.

Self-talk can also deal with the desire to smoke when you're feeling relaxed or happy. Increasing positive feelings may help — or use a little common sense, such as reminding yourself why you quit smoking, or "I've been successful so far, why blow it?" may be effective. And, of course, chew as much nicotine gum as you need to reinforce your self-talk.

Substitution. A way to stay off cigarettes is consciously to plan for whatever helps you most. For some it may be relaxation techniques such as deep breathing, or progressive muscle relaxation. There are tape cassettes with messages that are used in behavior-therapy clinics, such as the one by Dr. Richard S. Surwit at Duke University, that can be very helpful. Or just sitting in a quiet room, on a comfortable chair or sofa, or taking a soaking hot bath can work.

Or you may be the kind of person who has too much energy to enjoy passive relaxation — you relax better when you're physically active. If so, anything that involves moving around such as jogging, brisk walking, gardening, golf may do as much to relax tension as sitting quietly does for others.

Since for many people, the act of smoking is in part oral

gratification, just the act of chewing Nicorette will provide some of the absent oral pleasure of smoking. And, when not chewing gum, try munching low-calorie foods like celery, carrots, sunflower seeds, popcorn; or drinking tea, coffee (if your smoking habit wasn't strongly linked with that beverage) or fruit juices. Sucking hard candy works for many ex-smokers. One woman gathered smooth pebbles in her garden, washed them, and put them in her mouth. She called light-colored ones "vanilla" and dark ones "chocolate." While her mouth was filled with pebbles, she couldn't eat or smoke, and in this way outwaited her craving for a cigarette.

Assertion Skills. People who can assert themselves by refusing cigarettes, asking others not to smoke, or being able to seek help in a crisis have an extra defense against backsliding. The same kind of coping ability can forestall stress — by opting out of difficult situations such as being unafraid to tell your boss that you're being overworked. Assertiveness doesn't mean aggressiveness; it means being politely and quietly affirmative or negative about what you do or don't want.

Slip Recovery. Every ex-smoker is tempted to smoke; these temptations may be frequent and unavoidable. Many succumb and smoke a cigarette — but not all become smokers again. The difference is in their attitude toward what's happened, and their ability to deal with such almost inevitable slips.

On Shiffman's hotline, the most frequent calls were from people who said "I've blown my clean record," or, simply, "I've failed, I can't make it." Here's how to handle these seeming defeats:

Managing failure. Smoking a single cigarette after being abstinent for two weeks can be seen as total failure; or it may be perceived in the context of "I've already avoided smoking 420 cigarettes. Am I going to let this one wipe out that record?"

People who handle this kind of backsliding successfully often tell themselves, "This is bound to happen to many quitters. Okay, I've smoked a cigarette. This can teach me that, by not letting it throw me, I'm learning better how to deal with quitting."

Self-praise, not blame. Ex-smokers who give in to craving, can protect themselves from further relapse by recognizing that this difficult time requires exceptional self-respect. Instead of feeling guilty, you should reward yourself for the days or weeks you've not been smoking — buy yourself a new necktie or T-shirt, a pair of gloves or running shoes, or some other indulgence. It's not a recompense for not smoking, but a present for and to yourself because you feel good about yourself. This helps reinforce the new self-image you're building — of a nonsmoker.

Other techniques for overcoming slips may be relaxation, or physical exercise, discussed above under *"Substitution."* And don't be ashamed to chew more nicotine chewing gum. It's been prescribed for you to help you: *don't be too proud to use it as often as you need it.*

Situational analysis. Since every slip occurs under specific circumstances in the context of other events, ex-smokers who stay off smoking learn to analyze these factors and either avoid them or figure out ways of coping with them.

The vast majority of ex-smokers are, or have been, drinkers. Your biggest temptation to start smoking after you've quit is likely going to be alcohol. Having a drink almost automatically calls for smoking a cigarette. In one study, more than a third of smoking relapses occurred when the ex-smoker had been drinking alcohol, and nearly two-thirds when smokers were present. It's a cliché, but quite true, that alcohol releases inhibitions and undermines resolution:

an ex-smoker drinking with friends who smoke is exposed to nearly irresistible temptation. Knowing this, the wise quitter stays away from alcohol and smokers for at least a month or six weeks. And always carry a supply of Nicorette; a drink doesn't taste very good when you're chewing nicotine gum.

Changing life-style. Since smokers use cigarettes to manage situations, or for stimulation or relaxation, or as tension reducers, appetite suppressants, or simply as markers of changing behavior — say shifting from eating a meal to reading the newspaper, or marking different periods of the day — ultimately, giving up the smoking habit permanently means permanently changing one's life-style.

For many smokers, cigarettes mask or camouflage deepseated needs that they do not acknowledge. Rather than think about what they really want — it may seem unattainable — they reach for a cigarette. But if this is your case, when you've stopped smoking you can't do this anymore — you must face your real needs and purposes. To do this, you have to make a daily calendar of activities, and label each part of the day by whether it's spent in doing what you *want* or what you *should*.

A want is any noncompetitive behavior to which you can devote about an hour a day, something easy to do that doesn't demand much mental effort. Wants don't necessarily require company, but they must have some value to you, either physical, mental or spiritual. They may represent challenges to self-improvement, but must not be of a character that is likely to engender self-criticism if you "fail."

Shiffman says that many people smoke because they have an imbalance in their lives between *want* and *should*. Redressing the equilibrium between these two kinds of behavior can reduce the feeling of deprivation that leads to smoking.

It's impossible to define or list *want* activities — they're entirely personal. Whether a *want* for you may be sketching, running the marathon, washing the car, going to the movies, or playing the guitar — only you can know. But one thing about *wants* is strange: despite their obvious attractions, Shiffman says, "quitters often resist incorporating them into their lives, and may need substantial encouragement from a spouse, or a close friend, or spiritual adviser" — or, perhaps, this book.

All of the techniques Shiffman has identified as successful strategies by ex-smokers can be used by anyone who has quit, or wants to quit, cigarettes without professional help. But they don't preclude seeking help, such as joining a quit-smoking clinic. As we've said earlier, there isn't just one reason for smoking, there isn't only one kind of smoker, and there isn't just one technique to stay off cigarettes. But the basic strategies — and nicotine chewing gum — that work for other ex-smokers can be used by anyone who wants to quit smoking. And can make it possible to restructure an old habit into an entirely new one: not smoking.

What You Should Know
About the Author

WALTER S. ROSS is a Roving Editor of *Reader's Digest* who has written most of the articles about smoking in that magazine during the past fifteen years. He also created and edited *World Smoking and Health,* an American Cancer Society journal. Ten years ago, he published (via Reader's Digest Press) *You Can Quit Smoking in 14 Days,* which was endorsed by Dr. Luther L. Terry, former U.S. Surgeon General, and translated into five languages. He first reported on nicotine chewing gum in the *Digest* in 1980, when it was still an experimental drug product in the United States. When Nicorette was approved in 1984 by the Food and Drug Administration for prescription sale in the United States, he wrote an article about the gum for *Reader's Digest* at the request of the editors. He is convinced, like many experts in the field of smoking and health, that giving nicotine safely to smokers is the first important pharmacological advance in smoking cessation. That is why he has written this book, outlining a new quit-smoking program that utilizes nicotine chewing gum. Since it is the only product of its kind, it would be impossible to avoid describing it, or using its name. But this is journalism, not promotion: Mr. Ross has never had any financial interest in the gum. Neither he nor any member of his family has ever worked in any capacity for the laboratory that produces it nor for any of the companies that distribute it, nor owned any stock of these companies. He was retained only by the publishers of this book to write it. The contents are entirely his and their responsibility.

Acknowledgments

THE facts about smoking and health in this book come mainly from the various Surgeon General's Reports. There have been seventeen such annual reports since the first landmark *Smoking and Health: Report of the Advisory Committee to the Surgeon General of the U.S. Public Health Service* in 1964. In recent years, a number have focused on one facet of the problem; for example, the 1982 report dealt mainly with smoking and cancer. In 1983, the central pathology was cardiovascular disease, which includes heart attacks and strokes.

The author of this work has also consulted literally hundreds of separate papers on various subjects — more than thirty on the clinical trials of nicotine chewing gum, for example. For each of the *Reader's Digest* articles on smoking, from which material was drawn for *How to Stop Smoking — Permanently*, there were an average of fifty sources: not only papers published in professional journals, but interviews with the investigators and others. All of this material has been double-checked for accuracy and balance by the *Reader's Digest* research department, which routinely consults not only the author's sources but many others, to insure independent confirmation of both facts and judgments.

Reports of conferences on smoking by the National Institute on Drug Abuse have been extremely helpful, especially that on nicotine, published in 1979. Other excellent sources are the proceedings of various World Conferences on Smoking and Health, held every four years (most recently, 1983, in Winnipeg, Canada). The British Royal College of Physicians (London, England) has also published three reports that have affected international opinion, both professional and public. The International Union Against Cancer and the World Health Organization, both in Geneva, Switzerland, have issued many useful documents.

The author is deeply indebted to the *Reader's Digest* for the ability to research many facets of this subject in the United States and a number of European countries, and especially for permission to use the product of this research, which originally appeared in articles in the magazine. These articles include "Do You Know What Happens When You Smoke?" "Can Nicotine Help Smokers Quit?" "What Happens When a Smoker Stops," and "Nicotine Gum: The Drug That Helps Smokers Quit." He is also indebted to the American Cancer Society for its support in various editorial enterprises dealing with smoking and health: *World Smoking and Health*, an ACS journal which he edited for eight years, and several publications such as *Dangers of Smoking, Benefits of Quitting* (1980) and *Answers to the 50 Questions Most Often Asked About Smoking* (1982). Lawrence Garfinkel of the ACS is a world expert on smoking and health, generous with his information and opinions. The Cancer Prevention Studies, initiated by Dr. E. Cuyler Hammond and carried on by Mr. Garfinkel with the aid of more than 100,000 ACS volunteers, have been a rich source of epidemiological information on the effects of smoking.

Dr. Daniel Horn, former head of the National Clearinghouse on Smoking and Health, created the original quizzes on smoking motivation (grounded in the theories of Dr. Silvan Tomkins), on which the first four quizzes in this book are based. Dr. Karl-Olov Fagerström developed the quiz on nicotine addiction. The Office on Smoking and Health (as it's now known) has always been forthcoming with documents and information; special thanks to Robert Hutchings and Mses Fernandez and Murphy of that fine agency.

It would be impossible to name all of the international experts who have supplied information: outstanding are Dr. Michael A. H. Russell (England), Dr. Elvin Adams, Dr. Donald T. Frederickson, Dr. Ellen Gritz, Dr. John Holbrook, Dr. Julius B. Richmond, Dr. Nina Schneider, Dr. Saul Shiffman, all of the United States of America, Dr. Kjell Bjartveit (Norway), Dr. Kimmo Leppo (Finland), Dr. Lars Ramstrom (Sweden), Professor Theodore Abelin (Switzerland), Dr. Nigel Gray (Australia), Dr. Roberto Masironi (WHO-Switzerland), Professor Ferdinand Schmidt (Federal Germany), Mr. Michael Daube, formerly of Scotland and now in Australia.

Acknowledgment and thanks are due the Smoking and Health Program of the Canadian Department of National Health and Welfare in Ottawa for permission to borrow case history material from their excellent book *How We Quit Smoking*.

Needless to say, none of the sources consulted by the author is responsible for the use, interpretation or conclusions drawn from their material or interviews, nor for any errors or misinterpretations by the author. Since this book includes detailed discussion of a prescription drug tradenamed Nicorette, it is important for the reader to know that neither the laboratory that manufactures the medication,

Acknowledgments

A. B. Leo of Sweden, nor the company that distributes in the United States and Canada, Merrell Dow Pharmaceuticals Inc., participated in the preparation or publication of this book, nor do they endorse the views of the author.

Report of "Tar," Nicotine and Carbon Monoxide of the Smoke of 207 Varieties of Domestic Cigarettes February 1984

THE Federal Trade Commission's Laboratory has determined the "tar" (dry particulate matter), total alkaloid (reported as nicotine) and carbon monoxide content of 207 varieties of cigarettes. The Laboratory utilized the Cambridge filter method with the following specifications as set forth in the Commission's announcement July 31, 1967 and July 10, 1980:

1. Smoke cigarettes to a 23mm. butt length, or to the length of the filter and overwrap plus 3mm. if in excess of 23mm.

2. Base results on a test of approximately 90 cigarettes per brand, or type.

3. Cigarettes to be tested will be selected on a random basis, as opposed to "weight selection."

4. Determine particulate matter on a "dry" basis employing the gas chromatography method

published by C. H. Sloan and B. J. Sublett in Tobacco Science 9, page 70, 1965 as modified by F. J. Schultz' and A. W. Spears' report published in Tobacco, vol. 162, no. 24, page 32, date June 17, 1966, to determine the moisture content.

5. Determine and report the "tar" content after subtracting moisture and alkaloids (as nicotine) from particulate matter.

6. Carbon monoxide is determined by non-dispersal infrared spectrophotometer.

Concerning the 207 varieties tested, 15 were capable of being smoked to 23mm. The butt length of the other 192 varieties tested ranged from 23.8mm. to an average of between 41.5 to 43.0mm. The butt length of 171 of the 207 varieties tested exceeded 30mm.

The samples used were obtained by attempting to purchase two packages of each variety of cigarettes as distributed by domestic cigarette manufacturers during August 1982 through December 1982 in each of 50 geographic locations throughout the country. Not all varieties of cigarettes were available in each of the 50 geographic locations and in these instances, one or more additional packages of cigarettes were purchased in those geographic locations where respective varieties were available. The samples utilized in the tests were representative of the 207 varieties of cigarettes as available throughout the country at the time of purchase.

In the table listing the cigarette varieties in alphabetical order the "tar" and carbon monoxide content is reported to the nearest 0.1 milligram and the nicotine to the nearest 0.01 milligram, each with appropriate statistical values. The average weight is reported in grams per cigarette and the butt length range to the nearest 0.1 millimeter. In all other tables the average weight and butt length columns and the figures representing the standard deviation of the mean have been eliminated. The "tar" and carbon monoxide figures have been rounded to the nearest milligram (0.5 milligrams and greater rounded up, 0.4 milligrams and less rounded down) and the nicotine figures have been rounded to the nearest tenth of a milligram (0.05 milligrams and greater rounded up, 0.04 milligrams and less rounded down). Three tables respectively list varieties in increasing order of "tar" values, in increasing order of nicotine values and in increasing order of carbon monoxide values. Accordingly, "tar," nicotine and carbon monoxide figures in the tables represent rounded off averages without indication of their precision.

It should be noted that cigarette brands with assay results for "tar" and carbon monoxide below 0.5 mg. per cigarette and for nicotine below 0.05 mg. per cigarette are recorded in the accompanying tables with asterisks (*) indicating that they are below 0.5 mg. "tar," 0.05 mg. nicotine and 0.5 mg. carbon monoxide. The tables do not differentiate and no ranking is intended between these cigarettes because the current, approved testing methodology is not sensitive enough to differentiate between cigarettes at these levels.

On April 13, 1983, the Commission announced its determination that its present testing methodology for "tar," nicotine and carbon monoxide does not measure accurately Brown & Williamson's Barclay cigarettes and in fact understates the measured deliveries of these products. Therefore, it announced that until it adopts a new testing methodology that is able to measure Barclay cigarettes, future FTC Tar, Nicotine & Carbon Monoxide Reports will not include test results for Barclay cigarettes. As a result, no test results for Barclay cigarettes are included within this report. At that same time the Commission also found that there was a significant likelihood that the same problem (namely, an inaccurate reporting of the "tar," nicotine and CO delivery) existed with respect to Kool Ultra and Kool Ultra 100's, two other brands of cigarettes manufactured by Brown & Williamson. However, the Commission has not yet reached any conclusion whether Kool Ultra and Kool Ultra 100's are ranked inappropriately. Therefore, two asterisks (**) have been appended to Kool Ultra and Kool Ultra 100's in this report to indicate this continuing controversy.

Tar Nicotine and CO Content of Two Hundred Seven Brands of Domestic Cigarettes Tested by FTC Method
(Increasing Order of Nicotine)

Brand Name	Type	Tar 1	Nicotine 2	Carbon Monoxide 3
CAMBRIDGE	KING SIZE; FILTER; (HARD PACK)	*	*	*
CARLTON	KING SIZE; FILTER; (HARD PACK)	*	*	*
NOW	KING SIZE; FILTER; (HARD PACK)	*	*	*
NOW 100	100MM; FILTER; (HARD PACK)	*	*	*
CARLTON 100	100MM; FILTER; MENTHOL; (HARD PACK)	1	0.1	*
CARLTON 100	100MM; FILTER; (HARD PACK)	1	0.1	*
CAMBRIDGE	KING SIZE; FILTER	1	0.1	1
CARLTON	KING SIZE; FILTER; MENTHOL	1	0.1	1
NOW	KING SIZE; FILTER	1	0.1	1
NOW	KING SIZE; FILTER; MENTHOL	1	0.1	1
BENSON & HEDGES	REG SIZE; FILTER; (HARD PACK)	1	0.1	2
CARLTON	KING SIZE; FILTER	1	0.1	2
KOOL ULTRA**	KING SIZE; FILTER; MENTHOL	2	0.2	1
NOW 100	100MM; FILTER; MENTHOL	2	0.2	1
NOW 100	100MM; FILTER	2	0.2	2
KENT III	KING SIZE; FILTER	3	0.3	3
TRIUMPH	KING SIZE; FILTER; MENTHOL	3	0.3	3
ICEBERG 100	100MM; FILTER; MENTHOL	3	0.3	4
LUCKY 100	100MM; FILTER;	3	0.3	4
MERIT ULTRA LIGHTS	KING SIZE; FILTER	4	0.3	4
MERIT ULTRA LIGHTS	KING SIZE; FILTER; MENTHOL	4	0.3	4
MERIT ULTRA LIGHTS 100	100MM; FILTER; MENTHOL	4	0.3	4
TRIUMPH	KING SIZE; FILTER	3	0.4	3
SALEM ULTRA	KING SIZE; FILTER; MENTHOL	4	0.4	4
KENT III 100	100MM; FILTER	4	0.4	5
TRIUMPH 100	100MM; FILTER	4	0.4	5
DORAL II	KING SIZE; FILTER	5	0.4	3
DORAL II	KING SIZE; FILTER; MENTHOL	5	0.4	3
KOOL ULTRA 100**	100MM; FILTER; MENTHOL	5	0.4	4
TAREYTON LIGHTS	KING SIZE; FILTER	5	0.4	4
CAMBRIDGE 100	100MM; FILTER	5	0.4	5
CARLTON 100	100MM; FILTER; MENTHOL	5	0.4	5
CARLTON 100	100MM; FILTER	5	0.4	5
SALEM ULTRA 100	100MM; FILTER; MENTHOL	5	0.4	5
TRUE	KING SIZE; FILTER	5	0.4	5
TRUE	KING SIZE; FILTER; MENTHOL	5	0.4	5
VANTAGE ULTRA LIGHTS	KING SIZE; FILTER	5	0.4	6
VANTAGE ULTRA LIGHTS	KING SIZE; FILTER; MENTHOL	5	0.4	6
VANTAGE ULTRA LIGHTS 100	100MM; FILTER	5	0.4	6
WINSTON ULTRA	KING SIZE; FILTER	5	0.4	6
WINSTON ULTRA 100	100MM; FILTER	5	0.4	6
VANTAGE ULTRA LIGHTS 100	100MM; FILTER; MENTHOL	5	0.4	7
TRIUMPH 100	100MM; FILTER; MENTHOL	4	0.5	5

1 "Tar" — milligrams total particulate matter less nicotine and water per cigarette.
2 Nicotine total alkaloids reported in milligrams per cigarette.
3 Carbon monoxide reported in milligrams per cigarette.
* Indicates "tar" below 0.5 mg.; nicotine below 0.05 mg. or carbon monoxide below 0.5 mg. per cigarette.
** See statement in text concerning Kool Ultra brands.

Brand Name	Type	Tar 1	Nicotine 2	Carbon Monoxide 3
CARLTON 120	120MM; FILTER; MENTHOL	6	0.5	4
DECADE	KING SIZE; FILTER	6	0.5	5
DECADE	KING SIZE; FILTER; MENTHOL	6	0.5	5
BENSON & HEDGES ULTRA LIGHT	100MM; FILTER; MENTHOL; (HARD PACK)	6	0.5	6
BENSON & HEDGES ULTRA LIGHT	100MM; FILTER; (HARD PACK)	6	0.5	6
MERIT ULTRA LIGHTS 100	100MM; FILTER	6	0.5	7
BRIGHT	KING SIZE; FILTER; MENTHOL	6	0.5	8
CARLTON 120	120MM; FILTER	6	0.6	5
OMNI 100	100MM; FILTER; MENTHOL	7	0.6	6
PALL MALL EXTRA LIGHT	KING SIZE; FILTER	7	0.6	6
TAREYTON LONG LIGHTS 100	100MM; FILTER	7	0.6	7
MORE LIGHTS 100	100MM; FILTER; MENTHOL; (HARD PACK)	7	0.6	8
SALEM SLIM LIGHTS 100	100MM; FILTER; MENTHOL; (HARD PACK)	7	0.6	8
BRIGHT 100	100MM; FILTER; MENTHOL	7	0.6	10
VIRGINIA SLIMS LIGHTS 100	100MM; FILTER; MENTHOL; (HARD PACK)	8	0.6	7
CAMEL LIGHTS	KING SIZE; FILTER; (HARD PACK)	8	0.6	8
MORE LIGHTS 100	100MM; FILTER; (HARD PACK)	8	0.6	8
TRUE 100	100MM; FILTER	8	0.6	8
VIRGINIA SLIMS LIGHTS 100	100MM; FILTER; (HARD PACK)	8	0.6	9
SALEM LIGHTS	KING SIZE; FILTER; MENTHOL	8	0.6	9
TRUE 100	100MM; FILTER; MENTHOL	8	0.6	10
CAMEL LIGHTS	KING SIZE; FILTER	9	0.6	9
PARLIAMENT LIGHTS	KING SIZE; FILTER; (HARD PACK)	9	0.6	10
WINSTON LIGHTS	KING SIZE; FILTER	9	0.6	11
MERIT	KING SIZE; FILTER	9	0.6	11
MERIT	KING SIZE; FILTER; MENTHOL	9	0.7	9
BELAIR	KING SIZE; FILTER; MENTHOL	9	0.7	9
GOLDEN LIGHTS	KING SIZE; FILTER	9	0.7	9
GOLDEN LIGHTS	KING SIZE; FILTER; MENTHOL	9	0.7	9
GOLDEN LIGHTS 100	100MM; FILTER; MENTHOL	9	0.7	9
NEWPORT LIGHTS	KING SIZE; FILTER; MENTHOL	9	0.7	9
NEWPORT LIGHTS	KING SIZE; FIL; MENTHOL; (HARD PACK)	9	0.7	9
RALEIGH LIGHTS	KING SIZE; FILTER	9	0.7	10
BELAIR 100	100MM; FILTER; MENTHOL	9	0.7	10
KOOL LIGHTS	KING SIZE; FILTER; MENTHOL	9	0.7	10
VICEROY RICH LIGHTS	KING SIZE; FILTER	9	0.7	11
SALEM LIGHTS 100	100MM; FILTER; MENTHOL	9	0.7	12
VANTAGE	KING SIZE; FILTER	9	0.7	12
VANTAGE 100	100MM; FILTER	10	0.7	9
PARLIAMENT LIGHTS	KING SIZE; FILTER	10	0.7	11
BENSON & HEDGES LIGHTS 100	100MM; FILTER; MENTHOL	10	0.7	11
MARLBORO LIGHTS	KING SIZE; FILTER; (HARD PACK)	10	0.7	11
NORTHWIND	KING SIZE; FILTER; MENTHOL			

1 "Tar" — milligrams total particulate matter less nicotine and water per cigarette.
2 Nicotine total alkaloids reported in milligrams per cigarette.
3 Carbon monoxide reported in milligrams per cigarette.
* Indicates "tar" below 0.5 mg.; nicotine below 0.05 mg. or carbon monoxide below 0.5 mg. per cigarette.
♦ See statement in text concerning Kool Ultra brands.

Brand Name	Type	Tar 1	Nicotine 2	Carbon Monoxide 3
BENSON & HEDGES LIGHTS 100	100MM; FILTER	10	0.7	12
MERIT	100MM; FILTER; MENTHOL	10	0.7	12
VANTAGE	KING SIZE; FILTER; MENTHOL	10	0.7	13
MARLBORO LIGHTS	KING SIZE; FILTER	11	0.7	11
NORTHWIND 100	100MM; FILTER; MENTHOL	11	0.7	11
MARLBORO LIGHTS 100	100MM; FILTER	11	0.7	12
MERIT 100	100MM; FILTER	11	0.7	13
L & M LIGHTS 100	100MM; FILTER	8	0.8	5
L & M LIGHTS 100	100MM; FILTER; MENTHOL	8	0.8	6
L & M LIGHTS	KING SIZE; FILTER	9	0.8	7
PALL MALL LIGHT 100	100MM; FILTER	9	0.8	7
GOLDEN LIGHTS 100	100MM; FILTER	9	0.8	9
KOOL LIGHTS 100	100MM; FILTER; MENTHOL	10	0.8	9
NEWPORT LIGHTS 100	100MM; FILTER; MENTHOL	10	0.8	10
SATIN 100	100MM; FILTER	10	0.8	10
OLD GOLD LIGHTS	KING SIZE; FILTER	10	0.8	11
SATIN 100	100MM; FILTER; MENTHOL	10	0.8	11
RALEIGH LIGHTS 100	100MM; FILTER	10	0.8	12
VICEROY RICH LIGHTS 100	100MM; FILTER	10	0.8	12
LUCKY STRIKE	KING SIZE; FILTER	11	0.8	11
KOOL MILDS	KING SIZE; FILTER; MENTHOL	11	0.8	12
LUCKY STRIKE	KING SIZE; FILTER; (HARD PACK)	11	0.8	12
KOOL MILDS 100	100MM; FILTER; MENTHOL	11	0.8	13
MULTIFILTER	KING SIZE; FILTER	12	0.8	11
CAMEL LIGHTS 100	100MM; FILTER	12	0.8	14
WINSTON LIGHTS 100	100MM; FILTER	12	0.8	14
MULTIFILTER	KING SIZE; FILTER; MENTHOL	13	0.8	11
ALPINE	KING SIZE; FILTER; MENTHOL	14	0.8	14
PARLIAMENT LIGHTS 100	100MM; FILTER	11	0.9	10
REBEL	KING SIZE; FILTER	11	0.9	12
KENT	KING SIZE; FILTER	12	0.9	11
KENT	KING SIZE; FILTER; (HARD PACK)	12	0.9	12
LARK LIGHTS	KING SIZE; FILTER	13	0.9	12
L & M	KING SIZE; FILTER	14	0.9	13
L & M	KING SIZE; FILTER; (HARD PACK)	14	0.9	13
SARATOGA 120	120MM; FILTER; (HARD PACK)	14	0.9	14
MARLBORO	KING SIZE; FIL; MENTHOL; (HARD PACK)	15	0.9	13
MARLBORO	KING SIZE; FILTER; MENTHOL	15	0.9	14
GALAXY	KING SIZE; FILTER	15	0.9	15
VICEROY	KING SIZE; FILTER	15	0.9	17
SILVA THINGS 100	100MM; FILTER	12	1.0	9
SILVA THINS 100	100MM; FILTER; MENTHOL	12	1.0	9
REBEL 100	100MM; FILTER	12	1.0	13

1 "Tar" — milligrams total particulate matter less nicotine and water per cigarette.
2 Nicotine total alkaloids reported in milligrams per cigarette.
3 Carbon monoxide reported in milligrams per cigarette.
* Indicates "tar" below 0.5 mg.; nicotine below 0.05 mg. or carbon monoxide below 0.5 mg. per cigarette.
** See statement in text concerning Kool Ultra brands.

Brand Name	Type	Tar 1	Nicotine 2	Carbon Monoxide 3
PALL MALL LIGHT 100	100MM; FILTER; MENTHOL	13	1.0	12
EVE LIGHTS 100	100MM; FILTER	13	1.0	13
EVE LIGHTS 100	100MM; FILTER; MENTHOL	13	1.0	13
NEWPORT RED	KING SIZE; FILTER	13	1.0	15
NEWPORT RED	KING SIZE; FILTER; (HARD PACK)	13	1.0	15
EVE LIGHTS 120	120MM; FILTER; MENTHOL; (HARD PACK)	14	1.0	11
KENT 100	100MM; FILTER	14	1.0	12
LARK	KING SIZE; FILTER	14	1.0	13
LARK LIGHTS 100	100MM; FILTER	14	1.0	14
SARATOGA 120	120MM; FILTER; MENTHOL; (HARD PACK)	14	1.0	14
L & M 100	100MM; FILTER	14	1.0	15
TAREYTON	KING SIZE; FILTER	14	1.0	15
TAREYTON 100	100MM; FILTER	14	1.0	15
VICEROY SUPER LONG 100	100MM; FILTER	14	1.0	16
SALEM 100	100MM; FILTER; MENTHOL	15	1.0	13
CAMEL	KING SIZE; FILTER	15	1.0	14
VIRGINIA SLIMS 100	100MM; FILTER	15	1.0	14
VIRGINIA SLIMS 100	100MM; FILTER; MENTHOL	15	1.0	14
CHESTERFIELD	KING SIZE; FILTER	15	1.0	15
CHESTERFIELD 100	100MM; FILTER	15	1.0	16
KOOL SUPER LONGS 100	100MM; FILTER; MENTHOL	15	1.0	16
RALEIGH	KING SIZE; FILTER	15	1.0	16
WINSTON	KING SIZE; FILTER	15	1.0	16
SALEM	KING SIZE; FILTER; MENTHOL	16	1.0	14
WINSTON INTERNATIONAL 100	100MM; FILTER; (HARD PACK)	16	1.0	14
WINSTON	KING SIZE; FILTER; (HARD PACK)	16	1.0	15
MONTCLAIR	KING SIZE; FILTER; MENTHOL	16	1.0	16
MARLBORO	KING SIZE; FILTER	17	1.0	16
PICAYUNE	REG SIZE; NON-FILTER	18	1.0	14
SPRING 100	100MM; FILTER; MENTHOL	19	1.0	16
EVE LIGHTS 120	120MM; FILTER; (HARD PACK)	14	1.1	11
BENSON & HEDGES	KING SIZE; FILTER; (HARD PACK)	15	1.1	13
ST. MORITZ 100	100MM; FILTER	15	1.1	14
ST. MORITZ 100	100MM; FILTER; MENTHOL	15	1.1	14
KOOL	KING SIZE; FIL; MENTHOL; (HARD PACK)	16	1.1	15
LARK 100	100MM; FILTER	16	1.1	15
RALEIGH 100	100MM; FILTER	16	1.1	16
WINSTON 100	100MM; FILTER	16	1.1	16
NEWPORT	KING SIZE; FIL; MENTHOL; (HARD PACK)	16	1.1	17
BENSON & HEDGES 100	100MM; FILTER; MENTHOL; (HARD PACK)	17	1.1	15
BENSON & HEDGES 100	100MM; FILTER; (HARD PACK)	17	1.1	15
KOOL	KING SIZE; FILTER; MENTHOL	17	1.1	15
MARLBORO	KING SIZE; FILTER (HARD PACK)	17	1.1	15

1 "Tar" — milligrams total particulate matter less nicotine and water per cigarette.
2 Nicotine total alkaloids reported in milligrams per cigarette.
3 Carbon monoxide reported in milligrams per cigarette.
* Indicates "tar" below 0.5 mg.; nicotine below 0.05 mg. or carbon monoxide below 0.5 mg. per cigarette.
** See statement in text concerning Kool Ultra brands.

Brand Name	Type	Tar 1	Nicotine 2	Carbon Monoxide 3
MARLBORO 100	100MM; FILTER	17	1.1	15
MARLBORO 100	100MM; FILTER; (HARD PACK)	17	1.1	15
BENSON & HEDGES 100	100MM; FILTER	17	1.1	16
BENSON & HEDGES 100	100MM; FILTER; MENTHOL	17	1.1	16
NEWPORT	KING SIZE; FILTER; MENTHOL	17	1.1	17
PALL MALL	KING SIZE; FILTER	17	1.1	17
MORE 120	120MM; FILTER	17	1.1	20
KENT 100	100MM; FILTER; MENTHOL	15	1.2	13
MORE 120	120MM; FILTER; MENTHOL	15	1.2	18
PALL MALL 100	100MM; FILTER	16	1.2	15
HALF & HALF	KING SIZE; FILTER	17	1.2	16
OLD GOLD FILTER	KING SIZE; FILTER	18	1.2	18
CAMEL	REG SIZE; NON-FILTER	20	1.2	12
KOOL	REG SIZE; NON-FILTER; MENTHOL	20	*.2	14
CHESTERFIELD	REG SIZE; NON-FILTER	21	1.2	12
TALL 120	120MM; FILTER; MENTHOL	17	1.3	16
LONG JOHNS 120	120MM; FILTER; MENTHOL	17	1.3	18
LONG JOHNS 120	120MM; FILTER	18	1.3	19
PHILIP MORRIS	REG SIZE; NON-FILTER	22	1.3	13
MAX 120	120MM; FILTER	18	1.4	17
MAX 120	120MM; FILTER; MENTHOL	18	1.4	17
NEWPORT 100	100MM; FILTER; MENTHOL	20	1.4	19
OLD GOLD FILTER 100	100MM; FILTER	20	1.4	19
LUCKY STRIKE	REG SIZE; NON-FILTER	24	1.4	16
PALL MALL	KING SIZE; NON-FILTER	24	1.4	16
RALEIGH	KING SIZE; NON-FILTER	24	1.4	17
TALL 120	120MM; FILTER	19	1.5	19
ENGLISH OVALS	REG SIZE; NON-FILTER; (HARD PACK)	22	1.5	12
CHESTERFIELD	KING SIZE; NON-FILTER	25	1.5	15
OLD GOLD STRAIGHT	KING SIZE; NON-FILTER	26	1.6	18
PHILIP MORRIS COMMANDER	KING SIZE; NON-FILTER	27	1.6	15
HERBERT TAREYTON	KING SIZE; NON-FILTER	26	1.7	16
BULL DURHAM	KING SIZE; FILTER	28	1.8	23
PLAYERS	REG SIZE; NON-FILTER; (HARD PACK)	27	1.9	15
ENGLISH OVALS	KING SIZE; NON-FILTER; (HARD PACK)	29	2.1	15

1 "Tar" — milligrams total particulate matter less nicotine and water per cigarette.
2 Nicotine total alkaloids reported in milligrams per cigarette.
3 Carbon monoxide reported in milligrams per cigarette.
* Indicates "tar" below 0.5 mg.; nicotine below 0.05 mg. or carbon monoxide below 0.5 mg. per cigarette.
** See statement in text concerning Kool Ultra brands.